Novelist's Guide

THE
Novelist's Guide

POWERFUL TECHNIQUES
FOR CREATING
CHARACTER, DIALOGUE
AND PLOT

Margret Geraghy

PIATKUS

First published in Great Britain in 1995 by
Judy Piatkus (Publishers) Ltd of
5 Windmill Street, London W1P 1HF

Reprinted 1996

First paperback edition 1997

**The moral right of the author
has been asserted**

*A catalogue record for this book is available
from the British Library*

ISBN 0-7499-1441-6 (hbk)
ISBN 0-7499-1653-2 (pbk)

Set in Caslon 540 by
Action Typesetting Limited, Gloucester
Printed and bound in Great Britain by
Butler & Tanner Ltd, Frome, Somerset

Contents

Acknowledgements

The author gratefully acknowledges quotations from the following books:

Adams, Douglas: *The Hitchhiker's Guide to the Galaxy* (Pocket Books)
  The Long Dark Tea-Time of the Soul (Heinemann)
Aiken, Joan: *The Wolves of Willoughby Chase* (Jonathan Cape)
Amis, Kingsley: *Ending Up* (Hutchinson)
  The Old Devils (Jonathan Cape)
Amis, Martin: *Money* (Jonathan Cape)
  The Rachel Papers (Jonathan Cape)
Austen, Jane: *Pride and Prejudice* (HarperCollins)
Bennett, Alan: *Talking Heads** (BBC Books)
Block, Lawrence: *Telling Lies for Fun and Profit*
  (William Morrow, USA)
Boylan, Clare (ed.): *The Agony and the Ego* (Penguin)
Bradbury, Ray: *Dandelion Wine** (Hart-Davis)
  The Stories of Ray Bradbury (Granada Publishing)
Braine, John: *Writing a Novel* (Eyre Methuen)
Brande, Dorothea: *Becoming a Writer* (Macmillan)
Burack, Dorothea (ed.): *How to Write and Sell Mystery Fiction*
  (The Writer, Inc., USA)
Chandler, Raymond: *Trouble is my Business* (Penguin)
Cooper, Jilly: *Lisa & Co* (Arlington Books Ltd)
  Riders (Arlington Books Ltd)
Doyle, Roddy: *The Commitments* (Heinemann)
du Maurier, Daphne: *My Cousin Rachel* (Victor Gollancz)
Duncan, Lois: *The Twisted Window* (Hamish Hamilton)
Eco, Umberto: *Travels in Hyperreality* (Picador)
Egri, Lajos: *The Art of Creative Writing* (Citadel)

Acknowledgements

Ellin, Stanley: *The Man from Nowhere* (Jonathan Cape)
Ellis, Alice Thomas: *The Birds of the Air* (Gerald Duckworth)
Ellman, Lucy: *Sweet Desserts* (Virago Press)
Evans, Peter, and Deehan, Geoff: *The Keys to Creativity* (Grafton)
Forster, E. M.: *A Room with a View* (Edward Arnold)
Forsyth, Frederick: *The Day of the Jackal* (Century Hutchinson)
Fowles, John: *The French Lieutenant's Woman* (Jonathan Cape)
Francis, Dick: *Dead Cert* (Michael Joseph)
Frayn, Michael: *A Very Private Life* (HarperCollins)
Gardiner, Dorothy, and Walker, Kathrine Sorley (eds.):
    Raymond Chandler Talking (Hamish Hamilton)
Gawain, Shakti: *Creative Visualization* (New World Library, USA)
Goldberg, Natalie: *Writing Down the Bones* (Shambhala, USA)
Grisham, John: *The Firm* (Random Century)
    The Pelican Brief (Random Century)
Hardy, Thomas: *The Mayor of Casterbridge* (Macmillan)
Highsmith, Patricia: *The Talented Mr Ripley* (The Cresset Press)
Hildick, Wallace: *Children and Fiction* (Evans Brothers Ltd)
Keillor, Garrison: *Happy to Be Here** (Faber & Faber)
    'Post Office', in *Leaving Home* (Faber & Faber)
Kellerman, Jonathan: *Silent Partner* (Macdonald)
King, Stephen: *Carrie* (New English Library)
    *The Stand** (Doubleday, USA)
Koontz, Dean: *The Bad Place* (Headline)
Lawrence, D. H.: *Sons and Lovers* (Penguin)
Leonard, Elmore: City Primeval (W. H. Allen)
    Glitz (Viking)
Lodge, David: *Changing Places* (Secker & Warburg)
    Nice Work (Secker & Warburg)
Ludlum, Robert: *The Parsifal Mosaic* (Bantam Books, USA)
McCullough, Colleen: *The Thornbirds* (Futura)
MacDonald, John D.: *The Dreadful Lemon Sky* (Ballantine Books,
    USA)
McInerney, Jay: *Bright Lights, Big City* (Jonathan Cape)
Mansfield, Katherine: 'The Fly', in *The Dove's Nest and Other Stories*
    (Century Hutchinson)
Mather, Anne: *Duelling Fire* (Mills & Boon)
Moggach, Deborah: *Close to Home* (HarperCollins)
Mullan, Bob: *The Enid Blyton Story* (Boxtree)
Nell, Victor: *Lost in a Book: The Psychology of Reading for Pleasure*
    (Yale University Press)

Orwell, George: *Nineteen Eighty-Four* (Secker & Warburg)
Paice, Eric: *The Way to Write for Television* (Elm Tree Books)
Radway, Janice: *Reading the Romance: Women, Patriarchy and Popular Literature* (University of North Carolina Press)
Salinger, J. D.: *The Catcher in the Rye* (Hamish Hamilton)
Storr, Anthony: *Churchill's Black Dog and Other Phenomena of the Human Mind* (Fontana)
Symonds, Julian: *Bloody Murder* (Papermac)
Vine, Barbara: *A Dark-Adapted Eye* (Viking) Reprinted by permission of the Peters Fraser & Dunlop Group Ltd *A Fatal Inversion* (Viking)
Wibberley, Mary: *To Writers with Love* (Buchan & Enwright)
Zahavi, Helen: *Dirty Weekend* (HarperCollins)
Zuckerman, Albert: *Writing the Blockbuster Novel* (Little, Brown)

*Quoted material is from the Introduction to the book.

Introduction

How to Get the Best from this Book

> Novelists are not necessarily any more sensitive or
> perceptive than many of their readers; they are no
> nearer the 'front' of human experience than anyone
> else. What they have is a gift for representing what
> they see in such a way as to help us all to see better.
>
> *Alan Judd*

Writing fiction is an art. It isn't like medicine, accountancy,
or any other academic subject, where you work hard, pass
your exams and – hey presto, you're qualified. Yet many
How-to books would have you believe that writing can be
learned in a similar way, by memorizing rules and faithfully
applying them. The result, for many hopeful writers, is
disbelief and confusion when their precious manuscripts
come back with a paper-clipped rejection. What went
wrong?

What went wrong is that the writer relied too much on
the *mechanics* of writing and forgot about creativity. It's like
painting by numbers. It doesn't matter how carefully we load
our brush, how precise we are at following the instructions,
the final picture will never be art. Similarly, anything made

from a kit where we dutifully follow someone else's design is never a reflection of our own creative talent. The best it can show is our manual dexterity.

When I took over one writer's workshop, the students were deeply miffed when I refused to give them handouts. They had come to expect these from their previous tutor. I had a look at one of these handouts. The subject was 'Beginnings'. Included was a list of 'Functions':

1 It strikes the keynote
2 It introduces the main character
3 It sets the scene
4 It reveals the main character's purpose

These are all laudable aims. The reasoning behind them is impeccable. However, it's doubtful whether a writer trying to stick to them would come up with the following:

> The body lay on a small square of carpet in the middle of the gunroom floor. Alec Chipstead looked around for something to put over it. He unhooked a raincoat from one of the pegs and, covering the body, reflected too late that he would never wear it again.

This is the opening to Barbara Vine's splendid thriller, *A Fatal Inversion*. Although it certainly strikes the keynote, it neither introduces the main character, nor reveals his purpose, nor sets the scene. For that, the reader must wait until Chapter Two. Is this a bad beginning because it doesn't follow the rules? I don't think so. Rather, it's an excellent beginning from a writer who has learned to trust her instinct.

Don't misunderstand me. Rules have their place. But follow them blindly and you'll never sell anything. Indeed, it's doubtful whether rules can help at all until they've become a part of your unconscious. Can you imagine Shakespeare sitting down to write Hamlet with *Functions of the Beginning* propped up on his desk?

Writing to rule is the same as writing to formula, a recipe for dullness. It's an interesting fact that even books which appear to be highly formulaic are rarely perceived as such by their authors. This is easily explained. 'I've read Mills & Boons all my life,' says Sheila Holland, who has earned so much money from writing romances that she now lives in a tax haven. She, like many other authors, absorbed the formula as she read. She doesn't even have to think of it.

As long ago as 1934, in her book *Becoming a Writer*, Dorothea Brande identified what she termed the writer's 'dual personality':

> Like any other art, creative writing is a function of the whole man. The unconscious must flow freely and richly, bringing at demand all the treasures of memory, all the emotions, incidents, scenes . . . which it has stored away in its depths; the conscious mind must control, combine, and discriminate between these materials without hampering the unconscious flow.

The book you're now reading aims to develop the 'whole' writer. Although you'll find plenty of technique – and even the occasional rule – you'll also discover how to tap the power of your own imagination. Look out for the icons. They pop up whenever there's an idea, or a collection of ideas for you to explore. What they're saying is 'Over to you – give this a try.' You'll find some formal exercises, too. They'll help, but only if you do them! Once you can trust yourself, your own true voice, you won't need rules. You'll write better naturally. And what you produce will be fresh and original.

Who am I?

Finally, something about me and how I got started in writing and teaching. (It's OK, you can skip this if you want – I shan't be offended.) I had my first piece of fiction published when I was sixteen. It was a blatant piece of plagiarism, involving a scene from a B-movie Western at my local cinema. There was lots of dialogue along the lines of, 'Hey, boss, he sez if we don't walk outa here with our hands up, we won't walk out at all.' A newspaper printed it and sent me a postal order for five shillings (25p in today's money).

I should like to pretend that I never looked back, but that would be a lie. At nineteen, my writing got pushed to the back burner. I was a university dropout and – since my parents had gone abroad, leaving me with no home – I had to find a job fast.

A clothing store hired me as a management trainee. I started out on the lingerie counter, where I spent my days folding up bras and saying '34B? Certainly, Madam, try these for size.' I was soon fired, for having untidy hair, a scorched uniform (well, how was I to know that nylon melted on Mark 2?), and an inability to add up. I think the words used in my dismissal notice were 'poor attitude'.

But nothing is ever wasted. Years later, when I'd actually started making money from writing, a fictionalized account of that sorry time won me a prize in an autobiographical novel contest.

Like all writers, I've had my share of rejections – probably enough to paper Buckingham Palace – but the heady feeling of that first, early success stayed with me. Like the stubble-faced hero in my old dusty Western, I picked myself up and just kept on going.

The jump into teaching happened quite by chance. I'd been selling fiction fairly regularly when a man at my writers' circle pressed a bulky manuscript into my hands and asked me to read it. I was flattered – and nervous. I'd never seen an unpublished book before. The strange thing was that I could see what was wrong and how he could fix it. In return, he gave me a mug with a picture of New York on it.

I knew then that I wanted to teach, to have the satisfaction of helping other writers develop their talent. When an opportunity arose to run my own writers' group, I said, 'Yes, please.' Three years on, I cannot imagine life without it.

This book is a result of those three great years.

1

Two Techniques to Make You More Creative

In this chapter we're going to explore two techniques for stimulating and developing your imagination. These techniques weren't specifically designed for writers. They're stepping stones to creativity – which means you can use them in other areas of your life. So, even if, for some reason, you never finish that novel, you won't have wasted your time.

Throughout the book, I've suggested occasions where you might find these techniques particularly helpful. But feel free to use them whenever you want. The more you practise, the more powerfully they'll work for you.

Creative visualization and the power of the unconscious

Visualization is the technique of using your imagination to see pictures in your mind. There's nothing weird or mystical about it any more than there is about day-dreaming or becoming so lost in a book that you don't notice your surroundings.

Nor, despite its New Age label, is it new; we all use it every day of our lives without even noticing. For example, when we're outside in the cold, dreaming of being inside by the fire or soaking in a hot bath, that's visualization. It's also fiction, because until we actually get home and turn on the taps, that steaming bath exists only in our own imagination.

This is what story-telling is all about: turning something imagined into something real. It's therefore not surprising that studies of the thought processes of creative people show visualization is a key factor. In explaining his need to write, Jean-Paul Sartre once described his work as an attempt to 'pluck the pictures from my head and *realize* them outside of me'.

Enid Blyton, whose prolific output led some critics to suggest that she was actually a syndicate, saw all her stories in pictures. 'I make my mind a blank and wait – and then, as clearly as I would see real children, my characters stand before me in my mind's eye . . . the story is enacted almost as if I had a private cinema screen there.'

Similarly, Janet Dailey, an American author who can write a category romance in eight days, carries a 'filmstrip' in her head. 'I'm the director and the people already have their scripts. I tell them where to move. I can even reverse the filmstrip when I'm writing to see when they stood up and sat down.'

Don't get panicky if this doesn't sound like you. Until you've tried consciously to visualize, you may be unaware of how powerful it can be. If you're afraid you won't be able to do it, here is a simple visualization for you to try right now.

First, close your eyes and relax. Imagine coming home and noticing a strange smell the minute you step indoors. It's like turpentine or white spirit. You walk into the sitting room and surprise, surprise . . . someone has painted everything white. Not just the walls, but the curtains, the floor, the furniture, the cushions. Even the magazines and news-paper are smeared in bright white emulsion paint. The chemical smell catches in your throat. Tentatively, you step forward to open a window and your shoe sticks to the floor. Yuk, it's still wet.

Now, imagine leaving this room and going into the kitchen. Thankfully, this hasn't been painted. Everywhere smells normal. Can you remember the colour of the units, the position of the fridge, the hob? There's a lemon on the draining-board with a knife beside it. Imagine picking up that lemon, squeezing it, smelling it. Cut the lemon in half and bite into it. Some juice trickles on to your hand. The rest swirls around your mouth, runs freely over your teeth and down your throat . . .

When you've finished, pause a moment to reflect. This scenario isn't real, yet when you bit into that lemon, I bet your mouth began to water. Similarly, in some small corner of your mind, you could probably 'see' that white room. The thought process you used to conjure up these impressions is the same thought process you will use whenever you want to visualize.

The role of the senses

The visualization you have just tried owes much of its power to involvement of the senses. It isn't necessary to use all five senses in order to visualize. However, there's no doubt that sensory awareness enhances the vividness of your mental picture. Try removing the smell of the paint and the taste of the lemon and you'll see what I mean.

As you read through this book, you'll notice I mention the senses a lot. This is because they're vital for bringing fiction to life. Just as that lemon was made real for you when the juice hit your tastebuds, so your fiction will become real to your readers when they can feel the sun warm on their heads, the sand blowing in their faces, the crunch of grit in their tomato sandwiches.

Before we move on to something a little more ambitious, here's a brief glimpse of how visualization can help us in specific areas.

- *Characterization* Visualization enables you to share the 'stage' with your characters. In your head, you can move among them, deciding exactly what your viewpoint character can see. In this way, your characters will be real people, not just names on a page. Interestingly enough, Janet Dailey never refers to her people as characters: 'When I talk about my stories with readers, I notice that I'll say "Do you remember Chase Benteen?" I think of them as real people always.'

- *Scene and setting* If your scenes have no substance in your own mind, they won't have substance for the reader. If you can't see drizzle glistening in the light from a street lamp, the shadows cast by railings outside a park, the on–off flickering of a blue neon sign, neither can the reader. Visualization allows you to check your scenes as if you were actually there, making a note of details you might otherwise miss.

- *Plotting* Instead of thinking of your story in a vacuum, as a series of steps and possible situations, you can run a series of images through your head. Put your characters (or people!) on screen and get them to act out possible scenarios. Left to themselves, they may surprise you. They might even butt in and say something that you, as writer, had never thought of. As a result, your plot could take an unexpected turn.

- *Triggering your unconscious* Have you ever noticed how a name you thought you'd forgotten sometimes rises out of the blue? Or maybe you've gone to bed, worrying about a problem, only to wake up in the morning with the solution in your head? Or perhaps (more rarely!) a fully formed plot suddenly pops into your head? It feels like magic, but it isn't. The source is your unconscious.

Unfortunately, you can't force the unconscious to work for you. It's a bit like a soufflé. If you keep opening the oven door to see out how it's doing, all you'll achieve is a mess of soggy egg. Using visualization, however, you can coax your unconscious to deliver up its riches. This is because visualization induces a state of reverie and, as psychiatrist Anthony Storr points out in *Churchill's Black Dog and Other Phenomena of the Human Mind*, this is the state in which most creative discoveries are made: '. . . most new ideas or solutions to problems appear during states of mind intermediate between waking and sleeping'.

Preparing to visualize: three important steps

Choose a suitable time You can't get in the mood to visualize if there are children murdering each other in the next room or dogs barking to be taken for a walk. Choose a time when you won't be disturbed. If yours is the kind of house where the telephone is always ringing, unplug it (or buy an answerphone).

Relax The key factor in successful visualization, both for 'seeing' your fiction and for stimulating your unconscious, is relaxation. As Shakti Gawain says in her book *Creative Visualization:* 'When your mind and body are deeply relaxed, your brain wave pattern actually changes and becomes slower.' What you're aiming for is a kind of day-dreaming state because, as modern research shows, frequent day-dreamers possess greater potential for creative thinking.

For many of us, relaxing is often easier said than done. If this is a problem for you, don't worry. It will come. Try having a soak in a warm bath liberally laced with your favourite oil.

Afterwards, pour a glass of your favourite wine. Many of my students find the glass of wine particularly helpful!

Get comfortable Try a sofa, a bed, or, in the summer, a deckchair or sun lounger. Take time to settle yourself down and find a comfy position. Close your eyes. Take a few deep breaths and let them out slowly. Tighten your muscles, one at a time, and then consciously relax them. Screw up your forehead. Go on, do it really hard . . . and let go. Whenever you want to visualize, use these same three steps to put yourself in the mood.

Now you're ready to start.

An exercise in creating an inner retreat

In this visualization, I'm going to show you how to create an inner retreat, somewhere you can go whenever you want to be free of the real world. You may like to think of this as your special writing place, a secret corner of your mind where ideas, plots and characters are just waiting to be discovered.

I suggest you begin by imagining yourself at home, walking towards the closed front door of your house or flat. Pause for a moment in front of the door. When you open it, you're not going to see the usual scene. Instead, there'll be a winding path leading into a forest. Hold that image in your mind. Now open the door and step on to the path. As you walk down the path and into the forest, look around you. Notice the trees and the light of the sun slanting through the tall arching branches. Look at all the different greens.

Start bringing up the senses, one by one. Can you smell any fragrance? Perhaps the honeyed scent of gorse, or the tang of wild garlic? You choose; it's your visualization.

How does the ground feel beneath your feet? Is there moss growing around the base of the trees? Bend down and touch it. What does it feel like? Run your hand over the bark.

Is it smooth, or rough? What's on the ground? Dry leaves, pine cones, tiny blue flowers? If you want to pick them, go ahead. Take a long, slow, deep breath and notice whether the air is cool or warm as it enters your nose. Let it fill your lungs with the scents of the forest.

What can you hear? Wood pigeons? The faint crack of twigs as your feet carry you farther into the heart of the woods? Or perhaps somewhere ahead there's a stream trickling over smooth stones?

After a while, the trees get denser, more difficult to pass through, until eventually you come to a high gate. Beyond the gate is your writing retreat. Here are some suggestions as to what it might look like:

- A white clapboard summerhouse, with soft cushions on the floor and apples in boxes.

- A log-cabin with a fire in the hearth, resin-scented flooring, and patchwork quilts on the walls.

- An Elizabethan mansion with floor-to-ceiling windows and one of those polished oak staircases with a gallery above it and a cellar below. Just think of the fun you can have exploring all the rooms.

- An orchard full of peach and pear trees, and an old wooden seat beside a still pond.

- A small island fringed with coconut palms and pale sandy beaches, and with water so pure you can drink from the streams.

- A space ship, another planet, or an underground bunker with every comfort imaginable.

Use your imagination to create your own perfect place in your mind. Once you've created it, it's yours for keeps. You can come here at any time. And when you are here, you can have anything you want. And I do mean anything. The laws of the real world just don't apply.

You may want to stay a while. That's fine. You may even find yourself dozing off. That's fine, too. Whenever you're ready, gradually bring yourself back to the real world, knowing you can return.

When you've finished visualizing, write up what happened to you just as you experienced it and before the clarity has time to evaporate. Write in the present tense, and don't worry about grammar, punctuation, spelling or whether you're using the right words. Your aim is to get it all down while it's still fresh.

Later, take time to read through what you've written. Have you used all the senses? If not, you may also be neglecting them in your fiction writing. This means your writing won't be as vivid as it could be. Once you're aware of this, you can correct it. Put a little sign above your desk: REMEMBER SOUND (or whatever).

Problems with visualization

I don't know anyone who has used creative visualization and not found it an enjoyable experience. Occasionally, however, I come across someone who refuses even to try it. I remember one particular man who thought I wanted to send him on a psychedelic trip. He soon changed his mind when he saw its effect on the quality of other students' work.

Invariably, when people write down their first visualization, the prose is richer, more sensuous. Writers who have never bothered with imagery find it cropping up naturally as they strive to convey the exact nature of that sensory experience. One of my students, for example, described the tiles on a barn roof as being the colour and texture of thick shortbread.

I think what worries some people is the idea of 'losing control'. It's true that visualization is a mild form of self-hypnosis. But so is reading. Think for a moment what happens when you're engrossed in an exciting novel. Before you start, you know it's something the author has made up, but as the pages turn a strange thing happens. As the fictional world becomes more vivid, the real world recedes.

Victor Nell is a psychologist who has studied the similarities between reading and hypnosis. In *Lost in a Book*, he says that the most potent ingredient of many successful novels is 'trance potential' – meaning the extent to which the reader becomes 'a temporary citizen of another world' or 'falls through the page'. He has also discovered that readers' judgements of trance potential often override questions of merit and difficulty:

> '. . . although Tolkien's *Lord of the Rings* is a relatively difficult book, many readers prefer it to easier ones because of its great power to entrance; or for readers who usually avoid trash, a new Wilbur Smith, promising a rollicking good read, may be an irresistible temptation.'

As writers, our job is to present our readers with an alternative world. If we aren't willing to dream dreams and see visions, then no matter how we push and shove, our readers will never move farther than their comfy old armchair. So don't be put off. I promise you won't suddenly come to, wearing open-toed sandals and a beaded kaftan.

If relaxation is a particular problem, try a pre-recorded relaxation tape. There's quite a choice now and they're reasonably easy to find in big bookstores such as Dillons. I've found the ones produced by Potentials Unlimited particularly effective because they encourage you to build your own visualization while following the instructions.

You might also consider one of the Sounds of Nature tapes, specifically designed for visualization. The range includes gentle rain, waterfalls, waves and summer birdsong.

However, I must confess that one of my students thought the waves sounded more like chips spitting in hot fat.

At the time of writing, there's a wonderful shop in Neal's Yard, Covent Garden, London, which also produces music cassettes for 'relaxation and inspiration'. These tapes have lovely names, *Keeper of Dreams* and *Tranquillity*, for example. One, *Awakened Dreaming*, even claims to 'allow the listener access to their unconscious'. I can't vouch for its effectiveness. However, you can listen to any tape before you buy and there's a money-back guarantee should you decide later that you don't like it.

Don't get depressed if you're not immediately successful, either at relaxation or at visualization. As the road-digger said to the woman who wanted to know how to get to Carnegie Hall, 'Lady, you gotta practise.'

Creative search

As writers we are destined to be forever searching for the new angle, the fresh idea, the one brilliant thought that hasn't occurred to anybody else. I know it isn't easy. Every year, when I start a new writing class, students proudly present me with their precious fiction. They believe it's original. Indeed, some are astounded when I gently point out that the old Faustian theme of selling your soul to the devil is well past its own sell-by-date and needs a different twist to catch an editor's eye.

It's not just plotting that suffers. Cliché – a convenient word for non-original thought – is a virus which gets into everything: characterization, setting, language and style. I understand the problem. And the frustration. How is it possible to think of something that hasn't been done a hundred times before?

The answer is that we must cast our nets as widely as we

can – and then some. Forget normal thinking. Normal thinking tends to be linear, in that once your mind is running on a particular track it's like a wheel in a rut. Unless you make a conscious effort to break free, your thoughts are invariably going to be the ones that follow in a logical sequence.

For example, here's a list of ideas associated with the simple word 'potato':

varieties
growing conditions
physical attributes
ways of cooking (boiling, roasting, etc.)
recipes (duchesse, boulangère)
cut up and use as printing blocks

As each thought hits the page, we move to the next line, still thinking of potato – hence the term 'linear'. This approach may be fine if you're writing a textbook on potatoes, but it's the Black Death to fiction.

What's needed is a thought process that works in a non-linear way, that allows us to shoot off up side tracks, pursue blind alleys, maybe even scuttle backwards, in the hope of finding something that everyone else has overlooked.

That thought process is creative search. Unlike the list, creative search allows us to free-associate, to access patterns and images that may be lurking beneath the surface of our conscious brains. In *The Keys to Creativity*, by Peter Evans and Geoff Deehan, cartoonist Mel Calman describes his working methods. Note the sudden switch from linear thinking:

> I wrote down a whole lot of words, like . . . let's take rain, for example, 'cos it's always raining in England. And so you're thinking it's wet, you're thinking of duck's feet, you're almost free-associating. You're thinking of Noah's Ark, right? And you go through those and you think – well, I did Noah's Ark last time. Is there a fresh way to do Noah's Ark?

> . . . And then suddenly while you're doing that, you may
> think of a total tangential notion of . . . I don't know – some-
> thing quite different.

That going off at a tangent is the essence of creative search.
It's particularly important for fiction writers because it
breaks through the shell of rigid thought, putting us in touch
with what lies beyond the obvious, showing us connections
where none seemed to exist.

The best way to start is write a trigger word in the centre
of your page. For example, a creative search using our
humble potato, might look something like this:

As you can see, I got sidetracked by the mandrake which
reminded me of Iago's speech in *Othello*. It paid off. By the
time we get to the large forked root credited with human
attributes, that boring old potato sounds a good deal more
promising.

Each of the other satellite words could be explored in the
same fashion. It's like verbal doodling. When something new
strikes you, begin again at the centre. You can exhaust one
line of thought or have half a dozen going at the same time.

The more you do, the farther afield you go, the greater the chance of coming up with something unusual.

Using emotive words

Northrop Frye said that any word 'can become a storm centre of meanings, sounds, associations, radiating out indefinitely, like ripples in a pool'.

If we take something abstract, the word 'leaving', for example, we might start out as we did before, making verbal connections: leaving home, leaving school, etc. But 'leaving' is an emotive word. It conjures up associative images. And those images will always be unique to the person doing the search. If something is unique, it can't help but be original.

I'll use my own images of 'leaving school' as an example. When I was seven years old, my parents bought a business in another town. I came home from school every day, knowing no one would be home. The first time I did this, my mother left me a cold Cornish pasty, wrapped in greaseproof paper in the back porch. And, just so I'd have something to do while I was waiting, my father had cut the lavender hedge, leaving the sprigs for me to pick up from the damp grass. Even now, I can't smell lavender without remembering that day.

Consequently, were I doing this search, two of my connections would be 'lavender' and 'Cornish pasty'. What would yours be?

The buried images of your life

In the preface to *Dandelion Wine*, Ray Bradbury says: 'I was gathering images all my life, storing them away, and forgetting them. Somehow I had to send myself back, with words as catalysts, to open the memories out and see what they had to offer.'

Creative search is that catalyst. It can put you in touch

with the buried images of your life, the compost of your fiction. The following two exercises are designed to turn that compost.

A creative search exercise in colour

For most of us, colours are strongly evocative. They can spark recollections from long ago, a dress belonging to our grandmother, for example, a favourite toy, or the wrappings from an Easter egg.

Colour stirs the emotions. Think how many novels, films and songs use colours in their titles. Here are just a few: *The Red Badge of Courage*, *The Color Purple*, *The Scarlet Pimpernel*, *Blue Moon*, *The Lady in Red*, *The Lilac Bus*, *Goldfinger*.

Colour affects mood. One American writer, John D. McDonald, wrote a whole series of detective novels, all with such lurid colour titles as *The Dreadful Lemon Sky*, *Dress Her in Indigo* and *The Empty Copper Sea*. Similarly, Phyllis A. Whitney's romantic suspense novel *Vermilion* was inspired by the beauty of a red rock landscape.

Try using colour now in your own creative search. Write your chosen colour in the centre of a page and see what images come to mind. As soon as one surfaces, quickly write it down and wait for the next one. It doesn't matter whether you use nouns, adjectives, adverbs or short phrases to tag your thoughts. What matters is that you record them before they disappear. Don't reject anything, and don't worry if the page starts to look a mess. It's not for publication.

After a while, you may find that one image is particularly strong and you want to explore it in an actual piece of writing. Alternatively, some of your associations may have formed a pattern. Write something based on the pattern.

Student example

The writer of the example which follows abhors violence. Creative search on the colour red freed her to explore disturbing images. She completed both search and vignette in ten minutes.

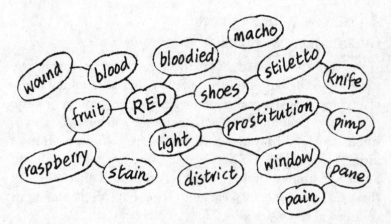

A red-bulbed fringed lamp silhouetted the woman in the window, her breasts thrust upwards by a white Wonderbra. In an ashtray beside her, smoke rose from a ruby-tipped cigarette.

Outside, the tall macho man pushed open the raspberry-red door, chipping off a few more flakes of paint, which fell to the ground and mingled with the rain. The woman tipped back her chair, crossing her ankles provocatively, placing her feet in their bright red stilettos on to the table. As the man entered, her head moved in negation. Her hair, wild as a forest fire, shook backwards and forwards across her face.

The man shouted and gesticulated, bent down and grabbed a shoe. The woman's crimson mouth arched as the stiletto, now a dagger, plunged deep into her breasts.

Blood gushed from the heel-wounds, spraying the man's face and his shirt with drops of warm, sweet burgundy. The man dipped his finger in the pool forming in her cleavage and drew a cross on her forehead.

Judy Smith

A creative search exercise in sensory awareness

We've already touched upon the importance of using the senses to bring our fictions to life. By the same token, many of our own most potent memories can be brought to the surface by exploring the images evoked by sight, sound, smell, touch and taste. For Marcel Proust, the sensation of biting into a *petite madeleine* elicited memories of childhood Sunday mornings when he and his aunt would dip cakes into their tea. That memory led to others. The result was eight volumes of *Remembrance of Things Past*.

The sense I've chosen for you to explore in this exercise is smell, but you can repeat it with all the other senses. In writers' workshops we usually start by doing a group creative search, focusing on the different kinds or categories of smells with a few general examples. Students then pick the smell, or smells, that seem most relevant to them.

When choosing a specific smell to write about, look for one that excites you, either by the vividness of the images associated with it, or by the feelings it provokes. If an unpleasant memory pops up, don't suppress it. Set it free.

In the following group search it was the reference to shoe repair that triggered Simon Heath's memory of his father's shop. He hadn't thought of it in years and was surprised by the clarity of his recollections. He then did his own creative search, using the shop as a nucleus. I'll show you both so you can see the progression.

Group search

Student example

The whole shop smelled of dust. It tasted of dust; you could let it settle on your tongue and feel the sediment as you transferred it to the top of your mouth. Then, leather, a lovely musty smell, reassuring and wholesome. Underneath that, a bitter, unpleasant odour of scorched rubber from the moulded heels, trimmed and shaped to fit the shoe.

But to me, my father's shop always smelled of paper bags, the coarse brown kind. My job was to bag the shoes, to place them heel to toe in the bag, and then, with a deft twist, to spin and seal the shoes into a parcel, then clip the ticket to the bottom seal. All paper smells, but especially cheap coarse brown paper, a smell that is neither pleasant nor unpleasant, but like the job itself, monotonous.

Simon Heath

Why does it work?

Well, I hope it did work for you. If you're not pleased with the results, don't worry. It could be that you tried to control the flow of your thoughts instead of letting them spill out. Creative search works when you think of it as opening all the doors and windows on a summer night. All you have to do is to breathe in the scents and let the sounds wash over you. You'll have plenty of opportunities to try again. For now, though, three thoughts to bear in mind:

• Starting at the centre means that you're not obliged to go in any particular direction. You have the freedom to explore without getting trapped. This is the path to more original ideas.

• When you're free-associating, the connections may at first be subliminal. If your thoughts seem random or nonsense, just go with the flow. It's a bit like watching clouds. If you watch long enough, you start to see pictures: a horse, a face, a man in a trilby. Alternatively, like Mel Calman, you may experience the light-bulb effect – a sudden moment of illumination.

• Don't reject any idea, however silly. The acceptance of thoughts that seem to lead straight into a brick wall is an important part of creativity. Some great discoveries have come about because people explored ideas that were at first failures. For example, someone at 3M developed an adhesive that didn't work very well. On one level, that adhesive was a failure. But not to Art Fry, another 3M scientist who discovered that the failed glue was just the thing to stop bookmarks falling out of his hymnal while he was singing in the church choir. The result was Post-It notes, a now ubiquitous accessory in every office.

When things don't seem to be working out for you, think, 'POST-IT NOTES!' and keep going.

2

Desperately Seeking a Cast of Characters

An American magazine once ran a quiz designed to tell readers whether they had the right qualities to be fiction writers. This was one of the questions: 'Do you sneak out in the middle of the night and sift through the contents of your neighbour's trash can?'

The right answer is, of course: 'Yes, I sift through my neighbour's trash because I'm just so curious about the way s/he lives.'

If dipping your hands into a mound of cold pasta, burst teabags and cigarette ash is not your idea of a good time, don't worry. It isn't necessary. However, the point behind the question is a good one. The one quality fiction writers cannot afford to be without is an insatiable curiosity about their raw material. In a word: people.

It sounds obvious. But how many of us actually study people, as opposed to just living among them? Imagine for a moment that you wanted to build a wall in your garden. You wouldn't just order a crate of bricks, and pile them on top of one another. First, you'd go out and look at a few walls.

And once you started looking, you'd quickly discover that they're not all the same. Brick patterns vary. Some are pretty, some plain. Bricks vary, too. The range is huge. What about mortar? What sand are you going to use? What cement? What sort of pointing? After a while, you'd find yourself telling people there's more to this building lark than meets the eye...

People – or playing cards?

There's more to people, too. Compared with that brick wall, we're light-years more complicated. Yet many first-time novelists plunge blissfully into the sea of human trauma, with not the foggiest notion of what makes people tick. The result, inevitably, is playing-card characters whose behaviour is strictly off-the-peg. When grief strikes, they feel the ground opening beneath their feet. Fright causes their hearts to hammer painfully in their fragile chests. Sadness brings out the hot, salty tears.

What makes real people *real* is their individuality, the way they *differ* from everyone else, not just in their appearance, but in the way they react. Oh, sure, they may cry when they're sad, but that's just one aspect of their response. There'll be something else too, peculiar to them. Take a look at this extract from D. H. Lawrence's *Sons and Lovers*. It's the scene in which Paul's mother dies:

> Suddenly Annie came flying across the yard crying, half mad: 'Paul – Paul – she's gone!'
>
> In a second he was back in his own house and upstairs. She lay curled up and still, with her face on her hand, and nurse was wiping her mouth. They all stood back. He kneeled down, and put his face to hers and his arms around her:
>
> 'My love – my love – oh, my love!' he whispered again and again. 'My love – oh, my love!'

> Then he heard the nurse behind him, crying, saying:
> 'She's better, Mr Morel, she's better.'
> When he took his face up from his dead warm mother,
> he went straight downstairs and began blacking his boots.

Well, there are tears here, as one might expect. But Paul himself doesn't cry. The real poignancy of the scene is his desperate repetition of the words 'Oh, my love', followed by his broken acceptance in the last line. If my mother died, I wouldn't go downstairs and clean my shoes. But I'd probably do something else equally idiosyncratic, and so would we all. This is the essence of characterization: touches of individuality sprinkled through our stories like cloves in apple pie.

Where do these touches of individuality originate?

From you – from me – from everyone living in the real world.

The watcher in the rye

There's only one way to find out about people and that's by observing them, not just when the whim takes us, but all the time. Unlike the rest of society, the writer is never off-duty. Whether we're at a dinner-party or a funeral, or sitting in the optician's, having our eyes tested, some small corner of our brains must forever sit apart, like a hidden black box, faithfully recording. Into that box will go the Freudian slips, the bad jokes, the dandruff, the smiles, the watercress stuck between a person's front teeth.

TV writer Eric Paice considers that this is a habit best formed in childhood: 'In any group of children . . . it's not difficult to pick the one most likely to make it as a dramatist. He (or she) will be the one on the edge, close enough to listen and watch but not so close as to be distracted by involvement in the activity itself.'

The sentiment is echoed by the American writer Alice

Hoffman. In the Long Island suburb where she grew up, there were, she says, no trees, no culture . . . no real sense of belonging. 'But then I never feel I belong; as a writer you're an outsider by nature.'

It's really only as an outsider that we can see people clearly. This doesn't mean we must be totally anti-social. On the contrary, we need to mix with people to 'fill up the well', as Hemingway put it. Just take care not to get so involved that you forget you're a writer. Try blending with the wallpaper from time to time. Avoid popularity. Popular people are busy people, and busy people have no time for writing.

Above all, never be pushed into being a club secretary or chairperson. Take note of Daphne du Maurier's comment that writers should be read – but neither seen nor heard.

A big bonus of people-watching is that no matter where you are, you need never be bored. Even the dullest situations – long speeches, queues in the post office, ritual gatherings – become interesting when you see them as source material for your novels.

Your own family can make a rich contribution to your writer's well. It's no secret that Johnny Speight based the TV character Alf Garnett on his father. Similarly, playwright Alan Bennett says that his ear for humour developed by listening to members of his family. In particular he remembers his mother's frequent references to 'common' people, a distinction he admits has seeped into his own way of thinking:

> There are some lace (or more likely nylon) curtains nowadays that are gathered up for some reason in the middle. They look to me like a woman who's been to the lav and got her underskirt caught behind her. They're absurd but that's not my real objection. They're common.

This brings us rather neatly to one of the best sources of character know-how: and that's you. Just as Alan Bennett has inherited a prejudice from his mother, so are we all products of a whole range of influences: not just our parents, but our social background, our religion, our schooling, even the books we read and the people we have as friends.

As an experiment, try looking at yourself as an outsider – perhaps another writer – might look at you. If, like Alan Bennett, you can bring yourself to be honest about your prejudices, your weaknesses, your peccadillos, you can use these in your writing. The bonus is that they'll come across as authentic, because when you *know* how something feels, you get it right.

You can mix and match experience and situation. For example, the writer of the film *Edward Scissorhands* used his own experience of being lonely at school to create a character whose physical appearance makes him an outsider. People who are different often feel excluded. The herd instinct drives us to associate with others of our kind, and if we are unable to do this, we are prey to insecurity. Maybe we're not good at games. Maybe our parents have just split up. Maybe we just don't have the right haircut.

Edward Scissorhands is an outsider because, in place of hands, he has scissors. His circumstances are undoubtedly very different from those of the writer, but that doesn't matter. Just as we can identify with Edward because we have all at some time known the edge of rejection, so the writer has used his own emotions to make the character believable.

Remember, too, that every character in your novel gains life through you – even the nasty ones. Every experience, every feeling, every action and reaction must be filtered through your consciousness before it reaches the page. Inevitably, this means opening your mind to thoughts and ideas for which you may have no sympathy. We can't fill our stories with clones of ourselves.

This doesn't mean that we have to give up our opinions. Rather, that a work of fiction must be fair to *all* its characters, not just the ones who share the author's point of view. Hemingway said that we should not judge, we should understand. This is the writer's integrity, and I know that many people have problems with it. How, for example, can we possibly share the mind of a murderer? We'll go into this later when we talk about the importance of identifying with our characters.

The blank–page horror

Although people-watching is such a vital step in creating flesh-and-blood characters, don't expect it to deliver the goods, neatly assembled and ready to go. It's true that real people are sometimes transported whole into the pages of a novel. However, the real value of studying people is to plunder aspects of humanity, a smile, a behavioural quirk, a viewpoint on life.

Sooner or later, you're going to encounter the blank-page horror. You know the scene: you've decided to start work on your novel TODAY, but the only thoughts in your head are, 'Oh dear, is that the time? I'd better go and walk the cat/wash my hair/get dinner/meet A at the pub/go to work/go to bed/fix that tap washer/iron a shirt/paint the ceiling.'

What's needed here are ideas, triggers, exercises to get us going when the muse won't co-operate.

Well, abracadabra! . . . See below for my top ten sources of character creation. Some will give you instant people. Some will show you how to build from scraps of information. Others, combined with creative visualization, will help you dig down into compost for that rich seam of gold. Try them all, then pick your favourites and use them regularly. Remember too, that different methods suit different writers. Don't be disheartened if they don't all work the same.

Creating characters:
top ten triggers

1 **Where are they now?** Think back to the place where most
of your characters start out in life. School. Schools are an
excellent source of material because within their walls is
society in a microcosm. Unlike adults, children haven't yet
perfected the façades that will mask them in later life. In
every school, there's always a bully, a show-off, a dark horse, a
sucker-up-to-teacher, someone who's generous, someone
who's mean, and someone who's always standing on the desk
with their back to the door when the teacher walks in – and
it's usually the same person. If you have one of your old
school photographs, fish it out. Study the faces. Then try
this exercise.

AN EXERCISE IN FACES

Choose one or two of those faces to write about, first as you
remember them, and second, as you imagine their lives
might be now. To get you started, make out a check list of
questions.

- What are they doing?
- Where do they live?
- Did they marry, and if so, what sort of person?
- Are they happy?
- How has life changed them?
- How much money do they make?

Remember: although the first part of this exercise is fact, the
second part must be fiction. The object is to start you fantasizing, so avoid choosing people you still know. Don't be
vague. Don't write: 'I imagine Charles is now working in
America because that's where he always wanted to go.' Try
instead: 'Charles lives on Arapahoe Avenue in Boulder,

Colorado. He gets up every morning, eats bacon and hash brown potatoes and drinks a double black coffee before driving to work in his new black Trans-Am.'

Alternatively, put Charles into a scene: 'On Saturday morning, Charles wakes early, walks into his peach-tiled bathroom and turns the shower on to "massage" . . .'

Let your imagination rip, based on what you remember. Try to think beyond the obvious. The bully, for example, the boy who thumped you in the stomach because he liked to hear you retch: he doesn't have to be a yobbo, cruising the streets for someone to pick on. He might have sublimated his aggression and become a gynaecologist.

When you've finished, take a look at what you've done. Compare the lengths of the fact and fantasy. Sometimes, when people do this exercise, the factual part is beautifully vivid. Then, suddenly, almost like a light being snapped off, the clarity goes. The content, too, becomes much more generalized, rather than specific. Creative visualization, with its emphasis on images, not words, is the technique to correct this. Really try to 'see' your character instead of thinking of him or her on an intellectual level.

2 *Zodiac people* This is a quickie. It'll give you instant characters when you're desperate, but they'll need work. Pop into a bookshop and either buy or browse through the horoscope books. Most shops have a good selection, one for each star sign, packed with information about character traits, health problems, tastes in food, sport and the opposite sex. Some will even tell you what you like in bed.

3 *Borrow an actor/actress/film star* This is a favourite with romantic novelists, many of whom stick a photograph of their hero on the wall above their desk. It's particularly useful for minor characters. In *To Writers with Love*, Mary Wibberley reveals that she 'borrowed' Margaret Rutherford for a sympathetic older woman, Burl Ives for a jovial uncle or

grandfather, and several other actors and actresses. The beauty of this technique is that the character has substance, but because you're working from the screen image, rather than a real person, there's not the same curb on your imagination. Nor, to my knowledge, has a writer ever been sued for libelling a character who's already fictitious!

4 **Choose a setting** Settings are effective as character triggers because they arouse our natural curiosity. (I dare you to walk down any street at dusk and resist those lighted windows!) A derelict Cornish mansion inspired Daphne du Maurier to write *Rebecca*. Similarly, P. D. James's *A Taste for Death* took an actual church in Oxford as its starting point. 'I always start my novels with a place . . . After that the characters emerge.'

The setting you choose could be anywhere. Here's something you can try:

AN EXERCISE IN SETTING

Use creative visualization for this. Get comfortable. Relax. Let your mind drift. When you're feeling pleasantly dreamy, imagine walking into your prospective character's bathroom. There on the wall is the medicine cabinet. What luck! Open it and take a good look at what's inside. If you have any trouble with this, think how much a stranger could find out about you by looking in your bathroom cabinet.

Always probe beyond the obvious. For example, you might start by deciding that your character dyes her hair, takes oral contraceptives and suffers from migraine. But look at the labels on the products. If they're all brand-name, it could be she watches a lot of television or reads magazines. What about her toothbrush? Is it clean and new-looking? Or are the bristles all flattened? A recent research study showed that poor dental hygiene is linked to low self-esteem. Dental floss and mouthwash could mean she's a high-achiever or, alternatively, a touch too fond of curry. Lots of out-of-date medicines? She could be a hoarder or a hypochondriac.

When you've finished browsing in the cupboard, you might want to look at the bathroom itself. Is the floor nylon shag, or hygienic tiles? Is there a tidemark on the basin? A fluffy cover on the loo lid?

What about the towels? In the film *Sleeping With the Enemy*, the position of bathroom towels is used to symbolize a character's paranoia. At the beginning, we see him straightening two towels so their edges are perfect, after which he beats up his wife. She escapes and moves to another State. Just before the climax, we get a shot of her bathroom . . . Uh-oh! Those towels are in line. We know then he's found her and is hiding in the house.

Remember, we are all revealed by the rooms in which we live, the things we put on our walls, the books on our shelves, even, judging by the phenomenal success of that TV commercial, our choice of coffee. It's our job as writers to look at these things and draw some conclusions.

5 ***What does your character want?*** Romantic suspense novelist Phyllis A. Whitney stresses the importance of knowing what every character wants *desperately*: 'The wants of different characters are going to clash, and if they are strong, powerful drives I'll have the beginnings of a page-turner.'

Makes sense, doesn't it? Wants drive us to action, and action is the lifeblood of a good story. Remember, too, that wants come in different flavours. There are personal wants – think of Hamlet driven to avenge his father's murder, Heathcliff's desire for Cathy, Cinderella's yearning to go to the ball. There are also wants arising from a particular situation – for example, all those thrillers in which the main character must disconnect the bomb, destroy the weapons factory or disarm terrorists before they kill innocent people.

What do *your* characters want? Love? Money? Success at work? Or perhaps revenge for some past hurt? Using creative visualization, try inviting your characters into your writer's retreat and asking them to tell you. Alternatively, you may like to do a creative search, using 'wants' as a trigger.

We're all prisoners of our hopes and needs. A story where the main character wants for nothing is a no-no.

6 *Jumping to conclusions* Remember when you were a child and made up cruel stories about someone you thought was a witch, or a spy, or a killer on the run? As writers we need to rekindle such vivid imaginings. Whenever you're in a traffic jam, sitting in a café, or even stuck in a queue at the supermarket, look around you. Who are those people in the next car (seat, checkout)? Is that man in the Ford Granada married to the woman beside him? Or is she his secretary? Perhaps they're co-owners of a local restaurant. She's telling him they should stop buying gateaux from their current supplier. He's arguing because he fancies the woman who runs the gateaux company.

Get curious. Start fantasizing. The image of a lone figure on the Cobb at Lyme Regis was John Fowles's inspiration for his novel *The French Lieutenant's Woman*. Baroness Orczy is reputed to have seen the Scarlet Pimpernel at a London train station. It was probably a trick of the mist, but who cares?

7 *Obsessions* Many famous fictional characters are based on obsessions or obsessional traits. Think of Dorian Gray's lust for youth, Scrooge's preoccupation with money or the jealousy of Othello. Obsessions are really just fears or traits that have got out of hand, and they're an excellent source of both

character and plot. I remember a chilling story about a woman who was so terrified of being murdered in her own home that she killed the gas man and hid his body in the cellar. For more inspiration, try reading Roald Dahl's short story, 'The Way up to Heaven', in which the main character is obsessed by time and can't bear to be late.

☀ This is a good opportunity to use creative search. Write the word 'Obsessions' on a clean page, and away you go. You can include your own obsessions, those of your friends and any others you've heard about.

8 **Revamp a type character** Type characters are defined by a single personality trait or social prejudice: the dumb blonde, the hard-as-nails businessman, the brisk but kindly doctor. Used straight, they're boring and unimaginative, but they can still be of use to us. The trick is to add particularizing – or contrasting – details. For example, a rural clergyman who also happens to be a motor-racing enthusiast has more interest-value than one who grows roses. A psychopath who collects dolls is different from what we expect and therefore more intriguing than one who sits at home reading Stephen King novels.

The question of stereotypes raises an interesting paradox. Research into the pulling power of formula novels shows that readers are comforted by the 'security' of familiar characters and situations. Contrary to what one might think, the stereotypical aspect actually heightens their response because it shows that everything's working as it should. It's like a pantomime: everyone loves the bit where the Dame shouts: 'Oh, no it isn't!'

This isn't a licence for trotting out stereotypes without modification. Rather we should aim for characters who appear fresh but are not so different as to make our readers feel uncomfortable. In other words, it's OK to serve steak every night, but make the sauce a surprise.

9 **Start a model file** Got a camera? Go out on location and take pictures of people who look interesting. London is a great place for this because it's multi-cultural. Don't just go for head-shots. Clothes and shoes can be just as fascinating.

Remember to be discreet, particularly if you're on holiday and want to snap the locals. In some countries, the camera is regarded as an invasion of privacy. My editor has a friend who was chased through the streets of Belize by a man with a machete after pointing a camera at a 'charming' local craftsman. The solution is to get yourself a telephoto lens – or, if you like the scent of blood, a pair of good running shoes!

10 **Steal a ready-made** Take any novel, pick an intriguing minor character and make up a new story about that person. This may seem like cheating but you'll be in good company. George MacDonald Fraser's famous Flashman is just one example of a character who first appeared in another author's novel. In Flashman's case, it was *Tom Brown's Schooldays* by Thomas Hughes. Fraser simply invented a set of fictitious Flashman memoirs detailing his adventures after leaving school.

There's nothing to stop you doing the same. In fact, odd as it may seem, there's no copyright in characters. However, if you want to use a *main* character from someone else's novel, it's probably sensible to head for the classics. If you then follow the example of the press and change names to 'protect' identity, readers will accept the character as your own invention. Which it will be when you've finished.

The kiss of life

I hope you find these triggers useful. Remember, though, that they are just *triggers*. The resulting creations will need work to make them walk, talk and breathe the same air as real people. This is something on which we cannot afford to skimp.

Someone once said that the true test of a character is whether you can imagine his/her off-stage life. Think of your own favourite fictional characters and you'll see that this is true. When readers like a character they want to know more. A letter to the author in *Raymond Chandler Speaking*, for example, asks all sorts of personal questions about his famous private eye, Philip Marlowe. His date of birth; his knowledge of perfume; his taste in films; his favourite brand of cigarettes; even whether he was an admirer of Orson Welles.

Similarly, in the preface to the uncut version of *The Stand*, Stephen King says that readers often 'discuss the characters as though they were living people, and ask frequently, "What happened to so-and-so?" as if I got letters from them every now and again.'

'Living' is how our characters should appear. The problem with many characters who fail to gel is that the writer hasn't taken the trouble to get to know them as people. This is a particular danger if you've been writing short stories, where in-depth characterization isn't so vital. Crime writer Ian Stuart remembers talking to an editor who suddenly asked, 'What sort of shoe polish does X use?' Stuart confessed that the question had never occurred to him. The editor then explained the importance of knowing 'everything' about your characters.

The point of this is not that readers need to know about our character's shoe polish, but that such details make the characters real to us. And, as Stuart puts it, a detailed picture 'enables you to introduce touches that give the depth and colour that bring a story alive. A seemingly casual reference to something in the past may explain a trait of character.'

The techniques writers use for getting to know their characters are many and various. Deborah Moggach suggests constructing their obituary from several different view-points: an old schoolfriend, for example, or someone who was in the Merchant Navy with them. Flaubert used to write warm-up scenes which never appeared in his novels. For many writers, it's hearing the character's voice that gets the pot boiling.

But perhaps the most important element is the one identified by Catherine Cookson: 'It's vital for you to believe in your characters. You have got to live them, to act them.'

Belief can only come when you see your character as someone with *feelings*. Actors do this as a matter of routine. They call it 'getting into the part'. Daniel Day Lewis, for example, went without food for several days to prepare for his role as a prisoner on hunger-strike.

We need to take the same trouble for all our main characters. It's a strange feeling, looking at the world through another person's eyes, but I think you'll like it. Use creative visualization to put yourself in your character's head.

Finally, here are some things for you to try, some areas to explore:

- For a few days, write your character's diary.

- Imagine how your character would behave in a range of ordinary situations: getting up in the morning, returning an item to a shop, cooking a meal, etc.

- To enter your characters' psyches, write their dreams. Where do they go in their non-waking hours? Perhaps they have a recurring dream, or a nightmare? Write these down. They will help to centre you in your characters.

- Put your character in a crisis situation – a bomb scare, a car accident, a lift stuck between floors. How would s/he react?

- If your character suddenly won a lot of money, how would s/he spend it?

- Make a list of your character's opinions on a range of subjects. Hint: choose ones on which you yourself have strong feelings. You never know, you may get into an argument!

3

Who's Telling the Story?

Point of view is a little like a damp patch in the corner of your ceiling. You can ignore it at first, but sooner or later, you just have to deal with it. The good news is that it's really not so scary.

Many writers have problems because they don't fully understand what viewpoint means. Let's start by clearing this up. In the real world, when we mention someone's point of view, we're talking about their *opinion* on a particular subject – cosmetic surgery, the best cure for a hangover or fixing that damp patch. Similarly, for the characters in your novel to appear like real people, they will also have to have opinions.

Point of view in novels is not about opinion. It's about focus, the angle from which the story is revealed. Suppose, for example, that a big jetliner develops engine trouble over the Atlantic and crash-lands on the sands of a holiday island. Miraculously, every one of the 350 passengers and crew survives. As they dazedly emerge, an out-of-work writer dumps her Piña Colada and rushes forward, notebook at the ready. What a story! And she'll get a different version, depending on whether she asks the captain, a flight attendant or someone stuck at the back beside the economy-class lavatories.

This is viewpoint. Although, technically, a novel about that air crash contains 350 possible points of view, the writer always limits that choice. For example, you might shine the spotlight on the co-pilot, Luke Travers, who has to take over when the captain has a heart attack (yes, it does happen!) Luke is now the viewpoint character and the story will concentrate on how the situation affects *him*.

But suppose, at some stage in Luke's story, the reader suddenly encounters this:

> Kelly Anne looked at Luke and was suddenly struck by how well he was coping. Although his uniform shirt was soaked under the arms, his face was calmer than the surface of a roped-off swimming pool. Gee, she thought, he's got more spunk than I realized.

This isn't Luke's viewpoint. He can't see himself sitting there looking calm and spunky. The story is no longer just Luke's version of the situation; it's Kelly Anne's too. What we have now is a double-viewpoint story. It's important to recognize when you're switching points of view. We'll talk more about that later. For now, though, here's a definition which you may find helpful: a viewpoint character is one whose thoughts, feelings and physical reactions the reader is allowed to share *at any given point in the story*.

Why do we need viewpoint?

A student recently handed me an outline he'd written. Terrorists had taken over a cottage and were planning an ambush. The owner of the cottage made a cryptic phone call which alerted the receiver, who, in turn, alerted the police. The police closed in and took the terrorists by storm. At the foot of the page, the student had scribbled, 'This doesn't grab me,' and went on to express surprise that he hadn't been inspired to turn it into a story.

I wasn't surprised. And, having read so far, neither should you be. Whose story is this? Does it belong to the terrorists? To the man in the cottage? The police detective? Or to all of these people? The answer is that we don't know. And until we do there's a limit to our involvement. Part of the pleasure of reading a novel is identifying with the characters, getting into their skins and sharing their experiences. Take a look at these publicity blurbs for published novels:

'Ex-SAS and on the run, Cranmer kills as easily and thoughtlessly as a trained assassin.' (*Dangerous Games*, by Julian Rathbone)

'On a cold spring morning, Cory Mackenson is accompanying his father on the milk round when a car appears before them and plunges into the lake.' (*Boy's Life*, by Robert McCammon)

'When Colonel Keane and his regiment are swept through a space-time warp to an alien land, he finds that only the power of rifles over swords and crossbows stands between them and destruction.' (*Rally Cry*, by William R. Forstchen)

All these novels sound exciting. They have another common factor. They're about specific, named people and the problems they face. In other words, they have a focus. Every successful novel follows this formula.

If *you* have a plot which doesn't seem to be working, take another look. It may be a viewpoint problem.

But hang on, you're probably thinking. Haven't we all seen films and TV drama-documentaries in which the camera flips from scene to scene, following the development of a *situation*, rather than the personal feelings of the characters? This didn't detract from our enjoyment. On the contrary, it helped build suspense.

You're dead right. But film and book are different media. In *Writing the Blockbuster Novel*, Albert Zuckerman says that in twenty years as a literary agent he has managed to place only one novel by a professional screenwriter. This isn't because screenwriters are bad at dialogue, plot or characterization. Where they fall short is point of view. In films, the only possible point of view is that of the camera, which is a detached observer rather than a participant in the events of the story. Novels are different. As Zuckerman puts it: 'What we enjoy most in a novel are often things that can never be physically seen. The authors about whom we become passionate delve deeply into the minds and hearts of a book's characters.'

Choosing your viewpoint

Viewpoint presents the writer with a lot of choices. Single or multiple? First person or third? Should there be a narrator? It's a bit like choosing a car. Do you go for the sun roof or the airbag? And what exactly *is* fuel-injection? I promise you, however, that time spent thinking about these options before starting to write won't be wasted. Your choice will affect not just the slant of the novel but the reader's emotional response to it.

Look at any story, and see how it alters with a switch of viewpoint. How about *Jack and the Beanstalk* from the point of view of a shy, reclusive giant who finds a trespassing little toe-rag has sneaked into his house? Imagine *Cinderella II*, the uncut version, in which we learn what it's like to be an ugly sister, hopelessly outmatched by a pouty-mouthed bimbo who thinks of nothing but clothes and marrying a prince. Similarly, the story of an adultery will have a different flavour, according to whether it's from the viewpoint of the faithful person, the naughty spouse, or, as in L. P. Hartley's

The Go-Between, the child who carries messages between the two lovers.

Let's now have a look at the different varieties of viewpoint and some things you might want to consider when making your choice.

Single-character viewpoint

In this viewpoint, the story is told from one angle only. You may have been warned to leave it alone because it's too 'restrictive'. A frequent objection is that the writer can't describe the viewpoint character's appearance without having him or her look in a mirror. Why? I don't have to look in a mirror to know what I look like, and I bet you don't either. It's true that unless you're trying to be funny you can't boast about how cute or pretty you are, but is that such a problem?

In fact, single-character viewpoint has a lot to recommend it. To make it easier for you to assess all the pros and cons, we'll split it into its three sub-choices:

First-person single viewpoint. Take a look at this extract from J. D. Salinger's *The Catcher in the Rye*:

> Where I want to start telling is the day I left Pencey Prep. Pencey Prep is this school that's in Agerstown, Pennsylvania. You probably heard of it. You've probably seen the ads, anyway. They advertise in about a thousand magazines, always showing some hot-shot guy on a horse jumping over a fence. Like as if all you ever did at Pencey was play polo all the time. I never even once saw a horse anywhere *near* the place. And underneath the guy on the horse's picture it always says: 'Since 1888 we have been moulding boys into splendid, clear-thinking young men.' Strictly for the birds. They don't do any damn more moulding at Pencey than they do at any other school.

When *The Catcher in the Rye* was first published in 1951, readers so believed in Holden Caulfield (the fictitious narrator) that they searched the streets in the hope of bumping into him. It's not hard to see why. First-person writing carries a natural ring of authenticity that's often missing in less intimate viewpoints. Salinger has exploited this potential by using the slang, exaggeration ('a thousand magazines'), and grammatical structures of teenage speech.

Here are some other reasons for choosing this viewpoint:

- It lends itself to a colloquial style, which engenders a feeling of cosy collusion. We're drawn into the character's confidence. As a result, we identify with him faster and start to see through his eyes. Consequently, we feel more in tune with him and his actions. We know a bit about his motives for behaving as he does.

- Because the writer is addressing the reader directly, there's no need for thought tags. This makes it good for stories of emotion, stress, or introversion, in which the main character needs to communicate his/her feelings.

- Because the style simulates speech, there's not the same temptation to slip into pretension, pomposity, or purple prose of the sombrous-night-descended-over-the-roseate-mountains variety.

- Characterization of secondary characters is easier because the observation comes straight from the viewpoint character. For example when Holden says of someone: 'He was the kind of phony that have to give themselves *room* when they answer somebody's question,' we know it's his point of view and we forgive him his bias. The same statement slipped into a third-person novel would sound like an author intrusion, a clumsy attempt to tell the reader what to think.

- It's a very natural way of writing. If you find it difficult to focus a story, to make it personal, switching to the first-person could make a dramatic improvement.

Now for the limitations:

- Frequent use of 'I' may make your character sound egotistical. You can combat this by avoiding 'I' at the beginning of sentences. It helps, too, to address the reader as 'you'. You may feel this is too chummy. However, there's no point in using the first-person if you want to keep the reader at arm's length.

- The only thoughts and feelings the writer can describe are those of the main character, who must be present in every scene (no popping down to the pub while he's having a snooze). In practical terms, this means you may have to think of more thoughts and feelings to attribute to one person. In a third-person novel, you can reveal two, three or more viewpoints on the *same* situation. This takes up more space. Consequently, a first-person novel has either to go more deeply into one person's psyche – or have more action in it.

Writers have developed little strategies for avoiding this last problem. *Twice Shy*, a novel by Dick Francis, is divided into two parts, each with a different viewpoint character, but both in the first-person. Susan Howatch used the same approach in *Penmarric* and *Cashelmara*. If this sounds odd, think of receiving a letter in which several people put in their fivepence-worth.

Third-person single viewpoint. As with first-person viewpoint, the story is still told from the point of view of one character; but that character is now referred to as 'he' or 'she'. This allows the readers to 'become' the character in a way that isn't possible in the first person. This is the viewpoint to go for if you want maximum reader involvement, because once the story gets going there are no disruptions, no changes of viewpoint to disturb the reader's concentration.

It's particularly suitable for genre novels with strong, action-packed plots in which the reader wants to share the main character's feelings. In Mills & Boon romances, for example, readers want to stick with the heroine and have sex with the hero. They're not too fussed about the hero's feelings about having sex with them. If he likes it, he'll tell the heroine and that's good enough.

Similarly, in tough-guy thrillers, male readers don't suddenly want to find themselves running down the street in a skirt and high heels. (Well, they might, but that's their business.)

However, this doesn't mean the viewpoint is no good for mainstream novels. Famous single-viewpoint novels include Kingsley Amis's *Lucky Jim*, and John Braine's *Room at the Top*.

Second-person single viewpoint. I know of only one novel written from this viewpoint, *Bright Lights, Big City* by Jay McInerney:

> You are not the kind of guy who would be at a place like this at this time of the morning. But here you are, and you cannot say that the terrain is entirely unfamiliar, although the details are fuzzy. You are at a nightclub talking to a girl with a shaved head.

In the eighties, there was a wave of interest in experimental writing, and if this viewpoint appeals to you the book is well worth reading. The effect is to put *you* the reader firmly in the main character's shoes. As such, it's a very intimate read. As with anything experimental, however, think twice before trying.

Third-person multiple Seventy-five per cent of mainstream novels are written from this viewpoint. This is the viewpoint with all the extras, including anti-lock brakes and cruise control. Do you want it? Well, you might. Here are some considerations:

- Are you aiming for a broad readership? With multiple (which applies to any number of viewpoints from two upwards) you don't have to choose between a male or female main character. You can have both, or several. You can write from the hero's point of view in one chapter and the heroine's in the next. This adds contrast and colour.

  In David Lodge's *Nice Work*, for example, the character of Vic Wilcox, right-wing working-class MD of Pringle's Engineering, is contrasted by that of Dr Robyn Penrose, left-wing feminist intellectual. When the two are thrown together, the radical difference in their outlooks provides the conflict for the plot.

- Does your story focus on a complicated relationship that may be more enjoyable for the readers if they can see it from different angles? For example, in *Close to Home*, Deborah Moggach uses five viewpoints to explore the potentially explosive dissatisfactions of two families living next door to one another. The wife of family 1 is attracted to the husband of family 2, as he is to her. The daughter of family 2 fancies the husband of family 1. The wife of family 2 is too preoccupied with her own life to notice what's happening. It's a novel in which no one says what they mean, and everyone has the wrong view of everyone else. This gives the book a feeling of movement that couldn't be generated by single viewpoint.

- Do you have several different plot threads, each of which needs to be supported by a different viewpoint character? For example, Stephen King's *The Stand* involves a killer plague that sweeps across America. The story tracks the experiences of isolated groups and the problems they encounter on their way to meet others. It would have been impossible to write this book from anything other than multiple viewpoint.

- Do you want to use viewpoint to add tension? For example, a story in which a young girl is kidnapped could switch between her viewpoint and that of the people trying to find her.

Although multiple viewpoint offers us the greatest freedom, it brings with it a crate of responsibilities. It's a bit like planning a party. Are you going to go for chipolatas on sticks, or a saddle of lamb with six sauces? Here are some things to consider before taking the plunge.

- Once you start following the actions of more than one character, you may have problems with chronology. For example, suppose you leave Melvyn fixing his car on Sunday afternoon. Now, you want to switch to his best friend, Pete, on Monday morning. When you go back to Melvyn, what day is it? Sunday or Monday? Or perhaps Tuesday? John Braine suggests that with a first novel it's best not to attempt more than you can perform: 'I personally didn't feel ready to deal with more than one character in depth until my sixth novel.'

- You have to be careful to balance the point of view. If one character is more interesting than another, readers may try to skip what they see as the boring bits. Similarly, if you write three-quarters of the story from one viewpoint and one-quarter from another, it might look like a mistake. Consider whether you shouldn't be writing a single-viewpoint story.

- With a lot of viewpoint characters, there's a danger of fragmentation. In a novel, as in real life, it's easier to identify with a few people than with a whole army. Ken Follett is a popular novelist whose books are all multiple-viewpoint. However, his early books, some of which contained over a dozen viewpoints, have disappeared into obscurity. It wasn't until he wrote *The Eye of the Needle* that he achieved a best-seller. He attributes this to his decision to concentrate in depth on fewer characters.

What's a sensible number? The simple answer is as few as possible. Imagine that you're paying these people to be your viewpoints – and you're on a tight budget!

- Finally, with more than one viewpoint, you have to make decisions about where to change the point of view. Many writers seem blissfully unaware of just how disruptive this can be for the reader. Imagine how *you'd* feel if you were suddenly yanked out of your own mind and into someone else's.

Handling switches

The easiest and best option is to save the switch for a new chapter, where a break occurs naturally. In *The Wrong Face*, a novel without chapters, Dianne Doubtfire indicates changes by putting a character's initial at the top of each section.

If you must switch in the middle of a chapter, always leave a gap. And make sure the reader knows who the new viewpoint character is. For example, if Tom, the present viewpoint, goes off to have a bath, readers will try to follow him. If you want them to stay in the bedroom with his girlfriend, you have to make this clear:

> 'Won't be long.' He brushed his lips across her forehead.
> *Now leave a gap.*
> Rachel watched Tom's disappearing back. It might have been nice, she thought, if he'd invited her to share. That would have been romantic, all that steam and horse-chestnut bath gelée.

We've now covered all the most common viewpoints, but there are others. I've left them until last because I didn't want to confuse you.

Narrator

This is the oldest viewpoint, a throwback to the days of oral storytelling when someone would sit in a group and simply tell a tale. Often, this would be something 'passed on' to the narrator by a person who'd been in the thick of it. It was a technique that worked because everyone could see who was telling the story.

After printing was invented, there was no role for the narrator. However, some written stories still resembled the oral ones. Henry James's *The Turn of the Screw*, for example, starts with a group of people seated around the fire telling ghost stories on Christmas Eve. The story proper doesn't begin until Chapter Two, the first chapter having been used by the narrator to create an atmosphere of suspense.

Nowadays, we take the view that if a story's worth telling, it doesn't need introduction. Nor do modern readers appreciate delaying tactics. Consequently, although narrator viewpoint still exists, its main purpose now is to co-ordinate the kind of story which can't be told in any other way. In Barbara Vine's *A Dark Adapted Eye*, for example, the main character is hanged for murder in the first chapter. The narrator is her niece:

> On the morning Vera died I woke up very early. The birds had started, more of them and singing more loudly in our leafy suburb than in the country. They never sang like that outside Vera's windows in the Vale of Dedham.

The technique is effective because the narrator was present during most of the important scenes, and can therefore act as the reader's eyes and ears. The chilling atmosphere is enhanced because neither we nor she really knows the full story.

However, a word of warning. If you're about to embark on your first novel, think twice before handling a story from the point of view of a minor character. Because Barbara Vine/ Ruth Rendell is such a brilliant author, she manages to make it work – and look easy. In fact, there's a very real danger that the readers may feel so detached from the action that they can't get involved.

Omniscient

This is another semi-redundant viewpoint. The author can look at characters from without and within, dip freely into everyone's mind, and then back off for objective description. In pure form, it's no longer popular. The constantly shifting focus stops the reader identifying with any one character. As a result, the reader feels outside the story, rather than within it.

However, in dilute form, omniscience is still used. For example, in a novel with a lot of viewpoint characters, you might want to introduce them all in Chapter One, and whet the reader's appetite with a brief glimpse into everyone's problems.

There are also occasions on which you might deliberately create a barrier between reader and character. Take a look at this extract from *The Day of the Jackal*:

> As Marc Rodin boarded his train, a Comet 4B of BOAC drifted down the flight path towards runway Zero-Four at London Airport. It was inbound from Beirut. Among the passengers as they filed through the arrivals lounge was a tall, blond Englishman.

This is omniscient because only an all-seeing being could know that these two events were happening simultaneously.

The Jackal, described here as a tall, blond Englishman, is an assassin with whom most readers wouldn't want to identify too closely. He is also an enigma, never identified by his real name. The viewpoint stimulates the readers' curiosity but keeps them at a distance.

You may have noticed something else. The passage sounds like something you might read in a newspaper, a colour supplement article in which the journalist has deliberately adopted a fictional approach. The effect is to give the story a touch of authenticity.

In fact, we never really share the Jackal's mind. In the scenes where he would logically be the viewpoint character, Forsyth employs yet another technique:

Detached viewpoint

From this point of view, the author acts as an impartial observer, faithfully recording what's going on, but never entering the character's mind. For the reasons given by Albert Zuckerman, it's not often used for a whole novel. A notable exception is Malcolm Bradbury's *The History Man*. The book consists of description and dialogue – which made it ideal for TV adaptation. However, according to David Lodge, who wrote an article about it in the *Independent on Sunday*, many readers 'found the text's refusal to comment, to give unambiguous guidance as to how its characters should be evaluated, disturbing'.

As with any unusual viewpoint, it's probably best left alone unless you know what you're doing.

Who makes a good viewpoint character

The viewpoint characters are the ones whose problems provide the storyline for the book. You, as writer, will need to spend time getting to know these characters as real people, developing their past, their present, and certainly their future. They are your stars. Make sure you can work with them. Here are some questions to help you decide.

- Which character or characters have the biggest emotional stake in the story, the most to lose if things turn out nasty? As Phyllis A. Whitney puts it, 'Small problems and small emotions never carry us far.' If it really doesn't matter to a character whether the by-pass is built, the murderer is found, or the plot is successful, discard that character and choose one who cares – passionately.

- Which character or characters are going to be most involved with the action of the story? It's hard to maintain the reader's interest in a character who's passive and does nothing to influence the progression of the story.

- Which characters are the most interesting? Viewpoint characters should be people whose thoughts and opinions the reader *wants* to know about. First, though, the character must interest you. Ask yourself: 'Am I going to enjoy looking at the world through this person's eyes? Or am I going to be bored?' If the latter, forget it and turn to someone else.

- Which characters are the most complicated? Complex characters are there to be explored. They're unpredictable. They have depth, which you – and the reader – will enjoy peering into.

Characters who don't make good viewpoints

- Characters with whom you, as writer, find it impossible to empathize. If you don't like your hero, you won't be able to make him likeable to the reader. And if the readers don't like him, they'll block your attempts to make them view the story through his eyes. Well, would *you* want to share skin and brain with a man who tortures rabbits?

This doesn't mean that your viewpoints must all be goody-two-shoes. However, if a viewpoint character is totally evil, with no redeeming features, the readers can't sympathize with his behavioural motives.

Patricia Highsmith is one writer who's succeeded with a 'bad' hero (try reading her Ripley books), but she couldn't have done it if she had hated Tom Ripley.

- Characters you don't understand. If you're a man who finds women more puzzling than a clock that strikes thirteen, don't try and write from a woman's point of view. Even D. H. Lawrence was caught out by this. In *The Plumed Serpent*, for example, a male character asks the heroine whether she regards sexual intercourse as spiritual or physical. Without a second thought, she replies that it's physical, 'of course'. In fact, for most women – certainly for women who love their men – sex is not just physical, but an emotional experience.

  Similarly, an ardent feminist, who's not interested in understanding men, might have difficulty doing justice to a male point of view. I once read a novel in which a group of women, disenchanted with their husbands, start a business. Good idea. If only the writer (or, in this case, writers) had stuck to the women's point of view. But they couldn't resist making one man a sacrificial goat. They take away his job, give him an apron, set him on a round of housework and babyminding, and then rub his nose in all his male failings.

  The result was a rather surreal piece of wish-fulfilment that didn't ring true.

- Characters who die before the end of the book. If a viewpoint character dies, you're asking the reader to die too. Most readers won't appreciate this. It can be done, but it's tricky.

An exercise in viewpoint

> It is a delicious thing to write, to be no longer yourself but
> to move in an entire universe of your own creating. Today,
> for instance, as man and woman, both lover and mistress, I
> rode in a forest on an autumn afternoon under the yellow
> leaves, and I was also the horse, the leaves, the wind, the
> words my people uttered, even the red sun that made them
> almost close their love-drowned eyes.
>
> *Gustave Flaubert*

The idea of seeing from the viewpoint of the sun may strike
you as a bit over the top. However, many writers have problems with point of view because they're just not able to leave
the security of their own heads. A lady once handed me a
story, supposedly written from the point of view of her
daughter-in-law, Ella, whom she didn't like. It contained the
following conversation between Ella and her friend, whom
we'll call Kate.

> Ella: I don't know what it is, but I just can't get on with her.
> Kate: If you ask me, you're not giving her a chance. She
> sounds a poppet.
> Ella: I suppose you're right. I really will try harder.

As you can see, poor Ella has been gagged because the writer
can't see the situation from her point of view. If we want our
characters to appear real, we must learn to see through their
eyes, even if that view conflicts with our own. As Wallace
Hildick puts it in *Children and Fiction*:

> To realize a character – to give it bones and muscles and
> sweat and blood and make it live – a writer must identify
> with it to some extent. Even if he is not predisposed to
> sympathize with a character he must at least try to see
> through his eyes, feel the way it feels.

The following exercise will give you practice in doing this.

Think of a relationship you've shared with another person, in which you feel there was a misunderstanding, disagreement or simply downright bad feeling. It could be a former lover, a friend, a person who bullied you at school. Try a creative search if you can't immediately think of someone.

When you've got a name, start a new creative search to trigger a scene in which to illustrate the situation and your feelings about it. Write about that scene from your own point of view.

The tricky bit comes next. Write about the situation from the other person's point of view, giving their feelings and reaction. It's important that those feelings are not the ones you would *like* the other person to have. To avoid this bias, use creative visualization to pretend that *you* are that person and you're seeing the world through his or her eyes. Relax, get comfortable and in your own mind *become* that other person.

It does work, I promise. One example that sticks in my mind was written by a male student who discovered that his best friend at school was gay. The realization had destroyed the friendship. For the first time, he tried to see things from the friend's point of view. The result was a piece of writing that moved me almost to tears.

4

Revealing Your Characters

Imagine a book entitled *101 Ways to Reveal Character*. Great, you'd say, lead me to it. Don't waste your money. After reading this chapter – or, more specifically, trying the next exercise – you'll be able to write that book yourself.

The truth is that you already know how characters reveal themselves. How can I be so sure? Because if you didn't, you couldn't form opinions of people in the real world – you wouldn't know what signs to look for, or how to interpret them.

For most of us, this process is pretty automatic. Which is why we're often not aware of it. For example, how often have you heard someone say, 'I don't know why, but I just don't like her,' or 'I can't put my finger on it, but I think he's trying to hide something'?

In the real world, character evaluation is rarely a rational procedure. It's based on a whole range of clues and messages that we transmit to others, often without realizing it. As fiction writers, we must train ourselves to recognize these subliminal signposts, as well as all the more obvious ones. With these in our armoury, we can then choose the most effective ways of revealing our characters to readers, secure in the knowledge that what works in life will work in fiction too.

The following exercise is designed to get you thinking more deeply about the ways in which we assess people. It isn't a one-off. Make a conscious effort to practise it whenever you meet or speak to someone new, until it becomes automatic. As we'll see later, it's often the small things, the nuances of human behaviour, that pack the biggest punch.

An exercise in people-watching

Start by drawing up a short list of people. Include the following for variety:

- A friend
- Someone you dislike
- Someone you've only just met or know only slightly
- Someone you see, but have never spoken to
- Someone you've spoken to on the telephone or heard on the radio.

For each person, the first step is to ask yourself what impressions you have of him or her. Try to identify all your impressions, not just one or two of them.

The second, and most vital step, is to pin those impressions down to actual sources. For example, don't say, 'Catherine is my best friend. I love her because she's always very kind.' Instead, think of some *particular* examples of Catherine's kindness. Maybe she once stuck up for you in an argument, or lent you her best ear-rings – and forgave you when you lost them.

You may find it helpful to do as one of my students did and set everything out as a table. For example:

John, a man I sometimes see at the pub.

Impression	Source of Impression
He's rich.	Drives a 7-series BMW. Lives in a posh area. His clothes look expensive. The label in his jacket says Savile Row.
A show-off, but also insecure. I don't know how he made his money, but I don't think he's used to it.	Always talking about his car, its power steering, its anti-lock brakes, its electric windows. When he's exhausted that, he moves on to his swimming pool – according to him, it's a necessity when you have kids and a wife who's at home all day. If he was 'old' money, I don't think he'd brag to someone like me. What would be the point?
Desperate for people to like him, but at the same time wants them to know that they're not quite his equal.	Insists on buying drinks for people he's only just met, and always urges them to 'have a double – I'm paying'.
Self-centred	Rarely asks questions. Doesn't really listen and butts in before you've finished.

| Vain | Always looks in the mirror on his way to the gents, checks his shoulders for dandruff. |
| Loves his children more than his wife. | Whenever you ask, 'How are your wife and kids?' it's always the kids who come first, never the wife. He refers to them by name. His wife is always just 'my wife'. |

Note: the conclusions this writer has drawn about John's personality indicate that he's male (the writer, I mean). The same behaviour directed at a woman might reasonably lead her to believe that John was trying to hit on her.

When you've completed tables for all the people in your list, it's time to move on to stage three of the exercise. Here, you take the sources of your impressions and classify them as techniques you can use to reveal your own characters.

In the above example, there are at least four broad categories: appearance, speech (dialogue), personal possessions, and action. But these can be split into all sorts of sub-divisions. Personal possessions, for example, include not just cars and houses but books, records and even pets. A man who walks a spaniel, for example, is very different from one who keeps piranha fish.

Possessions can be a simple indication of taste, but often they're much more, reflecting our feelings about ourselves and our position in life. In boasting about his car, for example, John is using it as a statement of his own worth: posh car equals man-to-be-reckoned-with sort of thing. In this extract from David Lodge's *Nice Work*, Vic Wilcox takes a rather different attitude to his rise up the ladder:

At Gran's house, a back-to-back in Easton with an outside toilet, you didn't go unless you really had to, especially in winter. Their own house in those days, a step up the social ladder from Gran's, had its own indoor toilet, a dark narrow room off the half-landing that always niffed a bit, however much Sanilav and Dettol his mother poured into the bowl . . . Now he is the owner of four toilets – damson, avocado, sunflower and white, all centrally heated. Probably as good an index of success as any.

Unlike John, Vic Wilcox does not sit in the pub bragging about his four toilets. Here, the writer has used a different technique, **interior monologue**, to show us Vic's feelings. Although there are no 'Vic thought' or 'thought Vic' tags, the voice is clearly his own.

In choosing lavatories, rather than cars or other more obvious manifestations of status, as an 'index of success', Vic shows us his matter-of-fact attitude to material wealth. To him, it's not so much a symbol as a reward for hard work. A reader can respect this. Consequently, he goes up in our estimation, whereas John goes down.

Because interior monologue reveals what people think, as opposed to what they may say or do, many writers consider it to be the most persuasive form of characterization. It also allows the reader to get closer to a fictional character than to anyone they're likely to meet in real life.

Sometimes, interior monologue takes the form of imaginary conversations in a character's head. In the next example, from Garrison Keillor's story 'Post Office', Bud has forgotten to put antifreeze in his pickup. See how Keillor uses the technique to draw the reader into Bud's world:

Bud wasn't about to take his frozen truck to Bunsen motors and become Clint's joke of the week, so he borrowed Carl Krebsbach's pickup and drove to Little Falls for a new radiator. But first he had to call Clint and say he was going. He

had to think of an excuse. 'I need to go to Little Falls to . . .'
To what? What could he say he was going to Little Falls to
get so that Clint wouldn't say, 'Oh, we got that right here.
What size you need?' Had to think of something too odd for
Lake Wobegon to stock but not too odd for Little Falls . . . a
chamfer bit. He'd heard of that somewhere; 'chamfer bit'
sounded good. Like something you ought to know, so Clint
wouldn't say, 'What's a chamfer bit?' He'd say, 'Oh, yes, we
used to have those but we don't anymore.' Unless Bud had
the name wrong. Maybe it was a chandler bit. And Clint'd
correct him. 'You mean a chandler bit.' And every time they
consulted him on mechanical problems, Clint'd remember
and say, 'Well, a *chamfer* bit might do the trick' and laugh
and slap his knee.

All this is going on in Bud's head. What it's doing for us is to
help us know Bud. We all have an inner life, a place to which
we retreat when we need to fantasize – or worry or grieve or
brood. If our viewpoint characters are to appear real, they
must be open to the readers. If they aren't, those readers will
feel excluded, get miffed, and lose interest.

Vary the exercise

You're not going to learn much about interior monologue by
studying other people. Instead, try a variation on the exercise you've just done. Take a book you've enjoyed, and write
down your impressions of the main character. See how many
of those impressions come from the character's own
thoughts.

Peeling the banana

So far we've talked about personal possessions and interior
monologue. If you've tried the above exercises, you'll now

have your own list of ways in which we learn about characters, both in real life and in fiction. One of the best ways is through dialogue, which we'll be covering in later chapters. Let's now take a spin through some other techniques. Oh, and in case you're thinking you might as well forget your own list and just rely on mine – don't. When it comes to characterization, there *is* no substitute for your own research.

Physical traits

Many How-to books will tell you that it isn't necessary to describe what characters look like. True. However, in real life (as you may discover when you try the exercise), most of us *are* influenced by people's appearance. And, rightly, or wrongly, we often draw conclusions about personality, sexuality, and even intelligence, based on physical traits. Consider the 'jolly' fat person, the high forehead of the intellectual, the jutting bust of the dumb blonde.

We wouldn't use such obvious stereotypes in our writing, but what we can take on board is the potency of the *image*. Let's look at two examples – the first from Jilly Cooper, the second from Raymond Chandler.

> Jake McInnes was a powerfully built man in his late twenties, with thick, dark hair, deep-set eyes the colour of mahogany and a very square jaw.

From this description, I think most of us can guess that Mr McInnes is going to get what he wants – because he's too cute not to. He's been designed for women readers who want a dollop of romance.

But hang on. What's so magical about deep-set eyes and a square jaw? Why do they work? They work because in the reader's mind they're *already* associated with male sexuality. Ever since Heathcliff strode through the pages of *Wuthering Heights*, the archetypal hero has been hard, dark and angular.

This doesn't mean you can't have a romantic hero who's as blond as a Viking and twice as dangerous. What it means is that such a man must stand alone because he can't trade on his forerunners. In a way, this gives him the potential to be a more exciting hero because people we don't know are always less predictable.

By contrast, you won't find the next character playing the hero in anything:

> He lay in the middle of the floor, still on his left side, a twisted, wizened, bald-headed little guy with drawn-back lips and teeth spotted with cheap silver fillings.

This man is a loser. Just look at the image evoked by those adjectives: 'wizened', 'bald-headed', 'little', 'cheap'. Someone who's already lost his dignity, his hair and the kernels of his teeth belongs on the floor and the reader knows it.

What both examples illustrate is the use of descriptive details as *symbols*, a kind of shorthand that the reader interprets without you having to spell things out. Let's face it, readers don't pick up novels to wade through the kind of detail you'd find in a police report. What they want is a few specifics to help them visualize the character. The writer's job is to be ruthlessly selective, to choose only those details that project the right image. If Jake McInnes has a boil on his neck, for example, we don't hear about it.

Similarly, in both examples, the brush-strokes are few. Once the image has been created, the writer doesn't hang around to tell us that the wizened little guy has dirt beneath his fingernails.

Symbolism is one of our most powerful weapons. The possibilities increase dramatically when we add clothes to our props cupboard.

Clothes

Unlike bat-ears and crooked noses, clothes are chosen by the characters – and that choice is revealing. A woman in a white silk shirt, for example, is very different from one in a pink, tie-necked blouse.

Unless you're setting your novel in a nudist colony, it pays to acquaint yourself with the images evoked by particular kinds of clothing. Start with the obvious ones: black leather jackets, denim jeans, crimplene dresses, Rolex watches, belted trenchcoats.

Learn to look at clothing with your writer's eye. What do they say about the people inside them? Don't forget shoes. A survey by one of the major shoe stores revealed that men who wear Oxford lace-ups are seen as honourable; those in country brogues are reliable; those in white shoes are con-men. Women who wear high heels are – wait for it – men-haters.

Remember, too, that we can't afford to dismiss the effect of social class on our character's taste. Put a character in a shell-suit, for example, and you're talking suburban lower-middle class.

This doesn't mean that we can't create characters who defy their appearance. On the contrary, this is one way of adding depth to a character. For example, in the TV series *Columbo*, the contrast between the main character's shabby mac and his brilliant mind adds piquancy to what would otherwise be just another detective story.

However, there's a difference between using appearance as a deliberate contrast, and slipping your romantic hero into comfy socks and sandals because you simply don't realize that as a sexual turn-on they're as useful as a surgical corset. The point about symbols is that they take effect whether we want them to or not. This applies whether you're writing a romance, a thriller or a literary novel. In the following extract from Martin Amis's *Money*, I'll leave you to find the symbols and decide if they're effective:

> As I feasted on my drink I sensed the hum, the confectionary of a feminine presence. I turned to find that a girl had joined me at the bar. Now she asked for white wine in her charged voice. New York is full of heart-stopping girls with potent colouring, vanilla teeth and these big breasts they all seem to be issued with as a matter of course.

Character tags

> Isidro had to stop so Teddy could take pictures of the entrance, like it was an historical place.
>
> 'That used to be the jail, 'ey?'
>
> He always said that, not 'hey', he said ''ey'. He was interested in everything he saw. 'The policia drive black and whites, 'ey?'

Character tags are idiosyncrasies – physical, behavioural or verbal – that make your character instantly recognizable. On their own, they're a shallow means of characterization, but they're very useful. In this example from Elmore Leonard's *Glitz*, once we know that Teddy says ''ey' instead of 'Hey' we can identify him the minute he speaks. This is particularly helpful in books where lots of characters could lead to confusion.

Tags can also alert us to a character's state of mind. For example, suppose you establish early that someone cracks his knuckles when he's feeling nervous. Later on, the character is speaking confidently, appearing to be in control, when suddenly, you let him crack his knuckles. Uh-oh, thinks the reader, is he going to fall apart? This increases the suspense.

Tags are also a great way to fix your character in the reader's mind. James Bond's shaken Martini is a character tag, as are Sebastian Flyte's teddy bear in *Brideshead Revisited* and Scrooge's 'Humbug' in *A Christmas Carol*. Similarly, I once read a book, the content of which has long since evaporated, except for one thing: the main character stubbed out cigarettes on his thumb. Cool, huh? Well, I thought so at the time.

☀ I recommend you keep a little file of tags. Everyone you meet is going to have at least one of them. And if you're short of ideas, just start with your own.

Exposition

Another name for exposition is gossip. In real life, we often know *about* people, before we know them personally. Someone will say, 'I've never met him face-to-face, but I hear he's absolute hell to work with.' Consequently, an exchange between two characters about a third can be highly effective in influencing the reader. For example, in Daphne du Maurier's *My Cousin Rachel* Philip receives a letter from his cousin Ambrose, who has married Rachel and is now living in her Florentine villa:

> 'I was never one for headaches,' he said, 'but now I have them frequently. Almost blinding at times. I am sick of the sight of the sun. I miss you more than I can say. So much to talk about, difficult in a letter. My wife is in town today, hence my opportunity to write.' It was the first time he had used the words 'my wife'. Always before he had said Rachel or 'your cousin Rachel', and the words 'my wife' looked formal to me and cold.

At this stage of the story, we haven't seen Rachel. In fact, it's another four chapters before she appears. By that time, the author has drip-fed us with information designed to raise our suspicions, along with the tension. This includes a technique we touched on in Chapter Two: using setting as a character trigger. Let's see how Daphne du Maurier uses setting to paint us a picture of the unseen Rachel.

Setting

Philip has arrived at Rachel's villa, hoping to find her there with Ambrose, only to discover that Ambrose has died and Rachel gone:

> The cypress trees closed in on us, and the shuttered villa, like a sepulchre, waited at the far end. As we drew closer I saw that it was large, with many windows, all of them blank and closed . . . The rooms all led into each other, large and sparse, with frescoed ceilings and stone floors, and the air was heavy with a medieval musty smell . . . I could not see Ambrose in this house . . . He could never have walked here with familiar tread, whistling, talking, throwing his stick down beside this chair, this table . . . Outside was a little court, a sort of cloistered quadrangle, open to the sky but shaded from the sun. In the centre of the court stood a fountain, and the bronze statue of a boy, holding a shell in his hands. Beyond the fountain a laburnum tree grew between the paving stones . . . The golden flowers had long since dropped and died, and now the pods lay scattered on the ground, dusty and grey.

I first read this book as a teenager and I remember its effect on me. Look at the images of death reflected in the words used: the villa like a 'sepulchre', the windows 'blank and closed', the 'dusty and grey' laburnum pods. These images, juxtaposed with others emphasizing the sheer foreignness of the place, the 'medieval' mustiness and the 'frescoed' ceilings, are transferred to Rachel, suggesting an aura of sinister strangeness. Bear in mind that this book was written in 1951, before the familiarizing influence of Thomas Cook.

Daphne du Maurier is just one writer who uses setting to reveal her characters. It's an effective technique because it serves two purposes. It helps the readers to visualize the scene, while at the same time allowing them to discover the character, instead of simply being told about him or her. As P. D. James says, 'Few things reveal the essential self more surely than the rooms in which we live.'

Body language

Have you ever watched *The Comic Strip* on television? One particular episode featured Peter Richardson dressed up as American actor, Al Pacino, who has been hired to play the part of Arthur Scargill in a drama documentary of the coal miners' strike. At one point, the screenwriter, played by Robbie Coltrane, hands 'Al' his script. Al glances at the first page, and drawls, 'I can say all this by the way I stand.'

That's body language: communicating without words, or rather without dialogue. Once you start using body language to reveal your characters, you'll find yourself resorting less and less to this kind of thing: 'Clare walked into the kitchen just as Billy was coming out. Billy looked so guilty that Clare wondered what he'd been up to.'

What's wrong with this? It tells us that Billy *looked* guilty. Just as 'Al' can convey a whole page of script by the way he stands, so Billy can convey guilt by a similar use of body language. He might hang his head, for example, shuffle his feet, or avoid Clare's eyes. The readers can then see Billy and think to themselves, 'Hey, I know what *that* means.' This is far more satisfying than simply being told.

There's another reason for using body language. What people say is often very different from what they feel inside. For example, if a character says, 'Right, Ted, couldn't agree more,' and then immediately folds his arms, Ted (and the reader) might reasonably suspect stormy waters ahead.

You'll find, too, that body language will allow you to punctuate dialogue with a few meaningful gestures instead of vague fumblings with ashtrays and coffee cups: 'Mother left the kitchen with one hand flat on her forehead and the other suspended in the air behind her' (*The Rachel Papers*, by Martin Amis).

Try this next time you see a play or a film. Watch the characters. See how their body language complements the dialogue or action – which it will, because the director will have made sure that it does. This is one way in which visual media compensate for lack of viewpoint – but that doesn't mean we can't cadge their technique.

Action

Actions speak louder than words. In fact, with the exception of interior monologue, actions speak louder than any of the techniques we've mentioned so far. The most memorable fictional characters are the ones we remember doing or saying things. We don't remember being told things about them.

Again, take a tip from the movies. When a character takes out a knife and chases a pretty girl through an alleyway, there's no need for a sign saying, 'This guy is dangerous'. And if the girl then wheels and cuts him down with a karate chop, we can guess that she's resourceful, brave and keen to survive. We can see it in front of us.

When to use action

- *Choose action to reveal characters whenever you find yourself trying to describe them in abstract terms* For example: 'Ben was an ambitious man. He wanted the good life.' 'Ambitious' is an abstract adjective. It's not vivid. It doesn't conjure up an image. Instead, think of something Ben could do to *manifest* his ambition.

Try creative search here to give yourself ideas.

You might, for example, show Ben admiring a Ferrari that he can't afford. He could be sitting at work, studying the Situations Vacant column and ringing one for 'High-flying executive'. Or, since ambitious people are often very pushy, he could be telling his boss about some grandiose scheme for doubling production on the shop-floor.

- *Choose action when you want to reveal characters in a subtle way* In literary novels, for example, where character development takes precedence over plot, the readers want to draw their own conclusions from what they observe. In this passage from Lucy Ellman's *Sweet Desserts*, the action tells us a lot about the main character:

> After making tea for myself and coffee for Jeremy, I unloaded all the shopping. One of my chief pleasures in life was dealing with store-bought food – all so virginally packaged yet bursting to be opened. I lined up a regiment of Jeremy's favourite yoghurts on the only shelf in the £7 fridge I'd bought at a Hampstead garage sale.
>
> I peeled open the one yoghurt I'd bought for myself, and tried it with my finger. Champagne Rhubarb. To go with my yoghurt and tea, I located the long stiff phallus of Fig Bars and extracted two, or maybe three. I hid these behind my yoghurt while I delicately re-aligned the plastic shrink-wrap around the remaining Fig Bars, sealed the wound with the Supa-Dupa Glue I'd bought for the purpose, and placed the deceptive packet on the top shelf along with the other biscuits and crisps I'd gotten for Jeremy (whose skinniness is one of the mysteries of this world). The stink of Supa Glue filled the kitchen as I started on the supper.

It's pretty obvious that this lady has an eating disorder. Although she talks only of her pleasure in dealing with food, her pathetic efforts with the Supa Glue tell a different story. There's a sexual element, too. Fig Bars aren't really phallic. The fact that she chooses to describe them as such suggests she might be using eating as a substitute for sex. Do you see

what's happening? Because there are no bald character state-
ments, we're encouraged to speculate, to interpret, to weigh
pros and cons.

- ***Use action to reveal changes in characters*** A reader
once told Jilly Cooper she'd enjoyed the way she could tell
that a particular character was going off her boyfriend: the
character had decided, when washing her hair, that he wasn't
worth conditioner.

   You can use the same technique to avoid a common fault
of beginners, that of characters 'jumping' from one
emotional plane to another. Real-life people often *appear* to
behave erratically, because we don't see the transitional
stages. In fiction, the steps must be shown. Readers will be
quick to notice small changes in any pattern of behaviour, be
it a plain woman who buys herself a flamboyant scarf, a sloth-
ful teenager who starts to help around the house, or a man
who decides to have an extra drink before dinner.

- ***Use action to point up a character's strengths or
weaknesses*** Nothing brings out the best or worst in us
more than a conflict that involves choice. In an episode of
the TV series *Northern Exposure*, Joel, the town doctor, is
worried about his Indian receptionist, Marilyn Whirlwind.
She's gone to Seattle in search of 'adventure'. Joel makes her
promise to phone when she arrives. When she doesn't, he
wants to go after her. But . . . there's a snag. He's broke, and
when he tries to borrow money he's told the term of his
contract will be extended to pay for it. This is bad news.
Joel's main aim in life is to work off that contract. The
choice is in front of him: Marilyn's safety? Or his own
freedom? The action he takes will define him for us. (He was
strong – he took the money.)

- ***Choose action to reveal contrasting characters*** Just
as an artist can make white look whiter by putting it next

to black, so can writers accentuate characteristics by contrasting one person with another. In *The Mayor of Casterbridge*, Hardy uses the preparations for a celebration to highlight differences between the mayor, Michael Henchard, and his employee, Donald Farfrae. Henchard, impetuous, extravagant and rich, organizes a grand hillside event with games and free food. Farfrae, practical and thrifty, but a touch thick-skinned, simply throws a few rick-cloths over some trees and charges admission for anyone who wants to dance. On the day, it pours with rain. No one comes to Henchard's games. Instead:

> All the town crowded to the Walk, such a delightful idea of a ballroom never having occurred to the inhabitants before . . . 'You see, Mr Henchard,' said the lawyer, another good-natured friend, 'where you made the mistake was in going so far afield. You should have taken a leaf out of his book, and have had your sports in a sheltered place like this. But you didn't think of it, you see; and he did, and that's where he's beat you.'

Henchard, deeply hurt, stays true to his impetuous nature and fires Farfrae on the spot. This is a perfect example of characters driving the plot instead of vice versa. If Henchard had been a different man, perhaps more laid-back, none of this would have happened. But it took a catalyst, a source of conflict, in the form of Donald Farfrae.

You can use the same technique in your writing. Lajos Egri is a Hungarian-American whose book *The Art of Creative Writing* is based on his wide experience as a playwright, teacher and Hollywood consultant. He maintains that one key feature of successful fiction is an unbreakable union between two entirely different types of character. As they struggle to break their bonds, rising conflict is generated: 'Take any one character and find his opposite, figure out why they can't separate, although that is the very thing they desperately wish to do, and you have a story.'

He's right. Although Henchard sacks Farfrae, he can't break free of him and the trouble between them continues to provide conflict until the end of the book.

 Why not experiment with some opposites of your own? Try the following:

Fickle – Loyal

Materialist – Idealist

Pessimist – Optimist

Gullible – Cynical

5

Do I Care about these Characters?

This is arguably the most important chapter in this book. A novel may survive many flaws, but if readers don't care about our characters, that's the end of our story. It's probably the end, too, if they take an instant dislike to the person or people we've chosen as our viewpoint. As Lawrence Block puts it in *Telling Lies for Fun and Profit*, 'To believe in them [the characters] and to get caught up in their fate is to spend time in their company and if they are unsympathetic, the prospect is unpleasant.'

This doesn't mean that we can't have nasty people in our stories. On the contrary, they're a necessary part of conflict, and later we'll be discussing some specific ways to make characters dislikeable.

The viewpoint character, however, is special. This, remember, is the person whose eyes, ears and feelings the readers will share as they travel through the book, or, in the case of multiple viewpoint, until someone else assumes the role. Our first task is to forge such a bond between this character and our readers that they no longer feel as if they're reading mere words, but have 'fallen through the page' and into the story. We call this process identifying with a character. If you mess up everything else, but achieve that for your readers, you're on your way to success. And here's how to do it.

Emotion: the key to reader identification

There's a tendency to scorn emotion as something a bit soppy. An emotional person is the kind who can't watch re-runs of *Dr Zhivago* without using up a box of Kleenex. Emotional people will invade your space and try to hug you in public. Women are often tagged as 'emotional' because they show their feelings, whereas men have been shamed into keeping them hidden.

In fact, emotion is a part of every single one of us. We may learn to control or suppress our emotions, but we can no more banish them than we can stop being human. Anger is an emotion. So are envy and jealousy. (You can find more listed in *Roget's Thesaurus* under Class Six, Affections.)

For us as writers, the important point to remember is that emotion is an invisible chain, linking people to people all over the world. In novels, it bonds readers to characters like chewing-gum to shoes. To show you how it works, I'm going to tell you about something that happened to me.

It was a Saturday evening, around seven o'clock. I'd spent the day in London, and before driving home I bought a cup of coffee on Richmond station. As I perched beside the counter, a train pulled in. The man sitting next to me jumped to his feet and went to hover by the steps leading down to the platform. I noticed he wore a bow tie and carried a huge bunch of flowers in florist's paper. A few moments later, he returned. Alone. So his girlfriend missed her train – there'd be another in a minute.

There was. But no girlfriend.

I sipped my coffee. The man began to wander around, apparently casual, except for too-frequent glances at his watch and the odd tug at his bow tie.

A third train arrived. She wasn't on it.

By now, my coffee was nearly finished. Unlike the man with the flowers, I wasn't waiting for anyone. There was nothing to keep me. But when the next train pulled in, I too scanned the passengers, looking for a woman who might be 'the one'. The man's face told me that she wasn't there.

Eventually, I had to leave. As I gathered up my parcels, a crowd of passengers flooded through the barrier. Again, the flower man rushed towards them. I could hardly bear to look. And then I saw her: a woman, all sleek hair and perfume, smiling the kind of smile we reserve for those we love. As the man's arms folded round her, I just caught his words: 'I was worried about you . . .'

And I'll tell you something – I almost stepped forward and said, 'Yes, and so was I.'

Why did I identify with this man? We had nothing in common. I'd never seen him before. The answer is that I did share something with him. I knew what it felt like to wait for someone who was late. Perhaps you, too, know the feeling, the anxiety, the worry? Or maybe the fear that they're not going to show?

That man's anxiety was enough to arouse spontaneous identification in me. In the same way, we, as writers, can trigger instant reader-identification with any one of our characters. Emotion is universal and timeless. When readers see a character being bullied, teased, hurt, humiliated, disappointed, emotionally threatened in any way, they cannot fail to respond.

Making a scene of it

Whatever kind of story you're writing, a thriller, a romance or something more literary, it pays to get the reader involved immediately. Straight narrative, in which you talk about your character's disadvantaged childhood, his misery at school, or his failed marriage, is never as powerful as what readers can see for themselves. For this reason, many novels start with an emotionally charged scene. In *The Thornbirds*, for example, here's how Colleen McCullough introduces Meggie Cleary:

> On December 8th, 1915, Meggie Cleary had her fourth birthday. After the breakfast dishes were put away her mother silently thrust a brown paper parcel into her arms and ordered her outside. So Meggie squatted down behind the gorse bush next to the front gate and tugged impatiently. Her fingers were clumsy, the wrapping heavy; it smelled faintly of the Wahine general store, which told her that whatever lay inside the parcel had miraculously been *bought*, not homemade or donated.

Inside the wrapping is a doll 'dressed in a crinoline of pink satin with cream lace frills'. The author allows Meggie her ecstasy. But not for long. Her two brothers appear, and despite Meggie's pleas, they wrench the doll from her and proceed to destroy it.

> . . . off came the dress, the petticoats and long, frilly drawers. Agnes lay naked while the boys pushed and pulled at her, forcing one foot round the back of her head, making her look down her spine, every possible contortion they could think of.
>
> [Finally] The doll's golden hair tumbled down, the pearls flew winking into the long grass and disappeared. A dusty boot came down thoughtlessly on the abandoned dress, smearing grease from the smithy across its satin.

Meggie is left scrabbling for the tiny clothes and pearls: 'the grief in her heart new, for until now she had never owned anything worth grieving for'.

That's the end of the scene. On the face of it, we have no more in common with Meggie Cleary than I had with the man on Richmond station. We're not four, we don't play with dolls, and most of us probably don't live in Australia. The only link is emotion. We all know what it's like to lose something we love.

Emotion crosses boundaries of race, sex, age, and even species. Take a look at this passage from 'The Fly', by Katherine Mansfield:

> At that moment, the boss noticed a fly had fallen into his inkpot and was trying feebly but desperately to clamber out again. Help! Help! said those struggling legs. But the sides of the inkpot were wet and slippery; it fell back again and began to swim. The boss took up a pen, picked the fly out of the ink, and shook it on a piece of blotting paper. For a fraction of a second, it lay still on the dark patch that oozed around it. Then the front legs waved, took hold, and, pulling its small, sodden body up, it began the immense task of cleaning the ink from its wings . . . It succeeded at last, and, sitting down, it began, like a minute cat, to clean its face. Now one could imagine that the little front legs rubbed against each other, lightly, joyfully. The horrible danger was over; it had escaped; it was ready for life again.
>
> But just then, the boss had an idea. He plunged the pen back into the ink, leaned his thick wrist on the blotting paper, and as the fly tried its wings, down came a heavy blot. What would it make of that? The little beggar seemed absolutely cowed, stunned, and afraid to move because of what would happen next. But then, as if painfully, it dragged itself forward. The front legs waved, caught hold, and, more slowly this time, the task began from the beginning.

This procedure continues until the fly is dead. The first time I read this out in a writers' workshop, one student was so upset, she asked me to stop. But hang on. This is a fly! Flies don't have emotions. Well, maybe not. But we do, and in that fly's place we know how we'd feel. In the end, we are all like that fly; we can't win against life. All any of us can do is the best we can.

You can use emotion to bond the reader to anything. The little alien in the film *ET* was the product of a special effects department, but his emotive situation had audiences the world over sniffing into their King Cones. Ray Bradbury wrote a story in which a baby is born, but, owing to a dimensional shift, it looks like a small blue pyramid. Bradbury hooks the reader's sympathy in a single line: 'The small blue pyramid moved. It began to cry.'

Opening your soul

Robert Frost said: 'No tears in the writer, no tears in the reader.' Before we can evoke an emotion for the reader, be it sadness, rage, jealousy or fear, we must first feel it ourselves. Theoretically, this should be a cinch. According to the developmental psychologist Piaget, by the time we're six, we've already experienced every human emotion. By adulthood, however, many of us have become experts at hiding our emotions behind our public persona. We may be unable – or unwilling – to bare our souls, even in the guise of a fictional character.

If this sounds like you, I urge you to stop and think seriously about your motives for writing. Fiction is the ultimate exposure of our private selves. While other people can provide us with outward behavioural signs, the source of our characters' inner baggage can only come from us.

A student once told me she had trouble giving a character a nasty streak, because she didn't know any nasty people. I gently pointed out that we bring nasty characters to life by searching for the nastiness within ourselves. If we refuse to acknowledge our dark side, insist that we're incapable of selfishness, maliciousness or negative thought, we simply can't build believable characters.

The following self-analysis exercise is one I offer to students whose viewpoint characters are wooden because their creator isn't allowing them to open up to the reader. Once we admit to ourselves that we have faults, that we're frightened of loneliness, that we hated our fathers, are jealous of our sisters, or once stole a cream cake, we can tap those veins to make our characters more human.

An exercise in self-analysis

First, relax. Go to the inner retreat you created in Chapter One. Now, think about yourself. What kind of person are you? This is the real you now, the one beneath the layers, the one behind the make-up, the wisecracks, the blue-tinted contact lenses. Here are some topics you might want to think about:

Regrets

Things that make me angry

Ambitions

A person, or people, against whom I hold a grudge

My obsessions

My weaknesses

Lies I have told

Things I won't admit to myself

Times I felt betrayed

People I've loved

People I can't like and why

Secrets

Emotions or feelings that cause me trouble

I want . . .

Fantasies

Alternatively, try selecting just one of these topics as a journal entry. Choose another one the next day and write about that. In her wonderful book *Writing Down the Bones*,

Natalie Goldberg talks about the benefits of sifting through the 'compost' of our lives:

> Our bodies are garbage heaps: we collect experience, and from the decomposition of the thrown-out eggshells, spinach leaves, coffee grinds, and old steak bones of our minds come nitrogen, heat and very fertile soil. Out of this fertile soil bloom our poems and stories.

You may find this exercise cathartic. That's a fringe benefit. Its real use to us as writers is that it opens our mind to experience we might be tempted to avoid. Best-selling author Betty Burton, for example, recalls a time when there were things she couldn't even talk about: 'When I was first married I lost several children at birth and I couldn't even mention it for many years. Now I can actually write about birth and death in my books because one day, I had to face it and do it.'

Please don't think I'm encouraging you to fill your novels with gloom and doom. Emotion is emotion, whether it makes the readers feel happy, sad, fearful or sexy. The point is that if something touches you very deeply, and you can convey that feeling to the reader, it will put power behind your words (remember *Edward Scissorhands*). Let's talk a bit about conveying that feeling.

Don't fake it

Feeling an emotion yourself and managing to conjure it up in the reader are two different things. One must come before the other, but the second doesn't always follow. This is hardly surprising. In the white heat of anger, for example, we may feel mad enough to throw plates, but it's just not the same when we're sitting at our desks with a cup of coffee and a chocolate digestive.

Similarly, passion and grief are powerful emotions which,

when we try to write about them, can slip into melodrama. The temptation is to over-write, to try and grab the reader with emotive words and phrases:

> When the vet had finished, Violet was sick with grief. [Suffering people always feel sick – or so we believe.] She wanted the ground to open up and swallow her. [We're trying really hard, here.] Tears poured silently down her face. [Tears must pour – shows the reader how much the character cares.] She had loved Carey with all her heart. [Just in case the reader didn't know.] And now he was gone. [Boo-hoo.]

You would never write such cliché-ridden rubbish? I'm pleased to hear it. However, the main fault in this is something more fundamental than mere cliché. Even if the author really had poured her heart on to the page, the passage would still fail to move us, because it concentrates too much on the character's own feelings.

You can't jump-start the reader like this. The trick, whenever you're writing about something that arouses strong emotion is to present the situation and let that do half the work for you. Let's have another go:

> When the vet had gone, Violet knelt down on the worn rug beside Carey's basket. He was still, his mouth slightly open, one ear bent over like a rose petal, revealing the pink skin inside. He smelt a little. Nothing bad, just the way you'd expect an old dog to smell. Violet stroked the fur on the back of his neck, scrunching it up, massaging his bald patches. After a while, she went into the kitchen, found a large black bin liner into which she scooped the three tins of dog food she'd bought at the weekend, Carey's food and water bowls, and his rubber toys with the teeth marks all over them. She stood for a long time, just holding the bin liner. In the end, she left it on the kitchen floor, and went

to run a bath. Cleanliness was next to Godliness. She'd always believed that. When the bath was full, she went back to Carey, gathered him in her arms, and gently, carefully, lowered the stiff little body into the warm water. It was, she reflected, the first time ever that he hadn't struggled.

OK, so it's turned out a bit sick. But then grief-stricken people often do things that seem sick to the rest of us. The difference between this and the first example is that here there's no abstract description of Violet's pain. The scene is tangible, concrete and specific, instead of vague and homogenized.

I mentioned passion, didn't I? In modern novels, this usually means sex. I could fill the rest of this book talking about the problems writers have in transferring sex to the page, but I'm not going to. Instead I'll tell one of the secrets. To write great sex, become a sensualist.

Tom E. Huff, a male author who by his own admission writes very sexy novels under a pseudonym, claims that the aura of sex, the sexual tension, is more important than the act itself. He achieves this by using the senses, all five of them, to make the reader *feel* what's going on. He cites the French novelist Colette as the most sensuous writer of all time:

> . . . the reader feels every subtle nuance of emotion because Colette has so skilfully prepared the senses. We feel the texture of old velvet and rough wood, we smell the stale face powder and sweat, we see the faded wallpaper and shabby Aubusson carpet, we hear the rustle of bedsheets and the short gasps of breath.

Similarly, for those of you interested in writing a romantic novel, Vivian Stephens, former editor of *Harlequin American Romance*, says that writers should work on arousing their own senses. Her suggestions include surrounding yourself with such sensuous accessories as scented candles and flowers, trying on expensive clothes made of silk, lace and satin, and sleeping between sheets sprayed with scented water.

In the end, though, sex is personal and the effectiveness of your sex scenes will depend upon whether *you* find them sexy. If silk and scented candles don't press your buttons, then by all means, chuck them away and hit the black leather jackets – or whatever else turns you on.

Think beyond the obvious. The movie *Ghost* got a 12 rating because someone had the bright idea of using a potter's wheel and a mound of clay to symbolize rising sexual passion. The result was a scene that was tactile, emotional and incredibly erotic.

You might like to try a creative search here to give you ideas for sensuous images and props.

Finally, here's an exercise in emotion designed for you to practise the techniques we've covered so far.

An exercise in emotion

First, relax and take yourself off to your inner retreat. When you're comfortable, go back in your mind to a time, or a fragment of time, when you felt something particularly strongly. I'll leave the choice of emotion up to you. It could be pleasure: the moment you suddenly realized you could swim, or tie your own shoelaces. It could be sadness, maybe breaking up with someone you loved. It could be anger, guilt or embarrassment. The most important thing is to think in images, to see the experience rolling through your mind, just like a film. Recall the sound, smell, touch and taste.

Now, using those senses, write a word-picture of that time. To enhance the immediacy, many of my students find it helps to write in the present tense. Aim at distilling the experience into the sensuous scene.

The beauty of this exercise is that you can practise it over and over again, with different emotions. Each time, if you can actually see and feel what's happening, you'll be much better able to translate the emotion into fresh, interesting language. Instead of resorting to clichéd metaphors and similes, you'll learn to coin your own.

Once you've had some practice in writing down your own emotions as you feel them, it's time to try the exercise with your characters.

It's important to remember that emotion affects perception and when our perceptions alter we behave differently. For example, if you've just fallen in love with someone you won't see their flaws. Similarly, you may have noticed that when you feel happy you can cope with all sorts of irritations. When you're upset, the slightest thing may have you snapping at people.

It's the same with fictional characters. If you don't know how they feel, you can't know how they'll behave. As a result, you may unwittingly try to shoehorn them into some line of action that's quite inappropriate. When this happens, the character will come across as shallow and unmotivated. Let's talk about this.

The role of motivation: why are my characters acting like this?

Lajos Egri said that motivation moves silently behind all personal turmoil. Consequently, it is a vital ingredient in every story. However, although we can usually find motives for our own behaviour, it's not so easy to discern the motivation behind the actions of others. This may lead us to believe that we can safely leave it out. We can't. If we don't know what's driving our characters, neither does the reader.

One of the pleasures of reading is getting so close to the main characters that we understand their behaviour as if it were our own. We don't necessarily have to agree with all their actions, but we need to know that there's something behind them. If the characters behave like robots, simply to fit in with the action of the plot, the readers will detect this and lose interest.

If you're having trouble with a character's motivations, the answer is to use creative visualization to 'become' that character. In fact, you should do this for all your characters.

First go through your routine for getting relaxed and dreamy. Get comfortable, get relaxed, and imagine yourself in your character's head. I find it helps to imagine myself possessing the character's physical attributes. Then, in the persona of your character, ask yourself some searching questions. For example: 'Why should I leave confidential papers on my hall table?' Or 'Why would I decide to walk home through the woods after missing the last bus?'

And if all you can think of is 'Well, otherwise there'd be no story,' you know that something needs fixing.

Lack of motivation is a particular danger in crime fiction. Someone handed me a story recently in which a postman, robbed of his mailbag, tracks down his assailants and accosts them in their lair. Would any sane citizen do something this stupid? Surely, he'd hot-foot it to a phone and let the boys in blue handle it?

Unless . . . the robbers made a threat. Suppose the postman is a former criminal, now going straight. Suppose he's recently married a woman who knows nothing of his past. But the robbers know, and they threaten to tell her if he goes to the police. Now, that postman has a problem. If he goes to the police, he risks losing his wife. On the other hand, if he doesn't tell the police how is he going to explain the missing mailbag?

Well, you get the picture. Dick Francis gets round the

problem of motivation by making his investigators normal people who are caught up in circumstances to which they must react. In *Dead Cert*, for example, the hero is a jockey whose friend dies after falling from a horse. The hero suspects it wasn't an accident, but he can't prove anything and so the police aren't interested. He is therefore forced to take matters into his own hands. Loyalty to a friend is a good motive for investigating a crime. So are revenge, self-defence and, in some cases, the pursuit of justice. Pure curiosity, *à la* Famous Five, is probably not enough.

If it's important for your plot that your character behaves in a particular way, try doing a creative search for a motive. In real life, people do appear to behave irrationally, but we can usually justify our own actions, however bizarre. Look for the reasoning and motive behind your characters' actions and the readers will stay with you.

For example, if a married man whose wife adores him starts having an affair, readers won't sympathize. On the other hand, if the wife is a domineering harpy who makes fun of him in public, readers will understand when he turns to a woman who makes him feel good.

How to make a reader dislike a character

Did you try the characterization exercise in Chapter Four? If so, you've probably got a few ideas of your own about what makes a person dislikeable. One of the most useful things to remember is that first impressions count. If a man comes into a room and the first thing he does is kick a dog, the reader will need no persuading that he's not a nice person. And first impressions stick. If, later, you reveal that the dog bit him while he was suffering from a migraine, the reader will say, 'No, no, he must have *provoked* it.'

Similarly, remember the boss in the extract from 'The Fly'? Any time you show a character causing suffering to others, readers will react with righteous indignation. Let's run through a few more possibilities in a creative search:

A dislikeable character might . . .

Break a promise (without good reason!)
Inflict physical pain
Be deliberately unkind
Behave selfishly
Sneer at goodness
Smell dirty
Have an unpleasant habit – pick his nose in public,
   etc
Pick on someone vulnerable ('Nobody roots for
   Goliath' – Wilt Chamberlain)
Lie or cheat
Blame someone else to save his own skin
Ignore a plea for help
Be weak ('Women do not like weak men, but they
   like men with weaknesses' – Chekhov).

Once you get started on a creative search, you'll find you have more ideas than you can cope with. Keep them for future use.

Adding colour to bit-part players

Every novel has minor characters, people who drift in and out when they're needed, people who open doors, serve meals, deliver parcels, and stooges whose main purpose is to listen patiently when the main character's talking through his theory of just why Miranda couldn't have been in the kitchen at the time of the murder.

Do I Care about these Characters?

Many writers don't bother to characterize walk-ons, people who appear once, or maybe twice, and then fade into the wallpaper. Other writers, such as Raymond Chandler, characterize everybody, even the dead guys. The trick here is put in a brush stroke, just enough for us to visualize how the character appears. Here are some examples:

- The clerk popped out from behind the glass screen like a chipmunk coming out of its hole.

- I sat on a stool and a hard-eyed bald-headed man behind the counter got up from a chair, wiped his hands on a thick grey apron, showed me a gold tooth.

- I waded over to the desk and put an elbow on it and was stared at by a pale thin clerk with one of those moustaches that get stuck under your fingernail.

- She just stood and looked at me, a long lean hungry brunette, with rouged cheekbones, thick black hair parted in the middle, a mouth made for three-decker sandwiches, coral and gold pyjamas, sandals – and gilded toenails.

The aim with this sort of description is to give the reader a sense of the character as a person. It works well for Chandler, and contributes a lot to the visuality of his stories, but don't overdo it.

Dick Francis is another author who takes the trouble to define his minor characters, often with a few simple traits: 'The two girls in the outer office looked at me expectantly. They wore tight sweaters and large quantities of mascara.' We've all seen girls like that. The effect is a pleasant feeling of recognition.

Similarly: 'The door opened and a nurse came in. She looked at me in pleased surprise and smiled. She had nice teeth.' In this case, the reference to the nurse's teeth is useful because it allows the author to refer to her again as 'the nurse with the nice teeth'.

In Stephen King's *Carrie*, he uses smell to give us an instant impression of a walk-on character: 'Norma led them around the dance floor to their table. She exuded odours of Avon soap, Woolworth's perfume and Juicy Fruit gum.'

If minor characters are going to reappear from time to time throughout the book, you want the reader to recognise them quickly. Character tags are the answer. In Jilly Cooper's *Riders*, for example, Lavinia Greenslade can't pronounce her 'Rs'. 'Come and have a dwink,' she says, and 'Would you like to share my wice and chicken?' It's a neat touch and it works. We know who's talking without being told.

Finally, an unusual name will help to fix a character in the reader's memory banks. Charles Dickens was the master at this. Who could forget Uriah Heep? Similarly, try a nickname that tells the reader something about the character. In Charlotte Bingham's *Country Life*, for example, the Mu-Mu maiden is a woman who wears mules. In the TV series *Mash*, Radar was a character who often knew what was going to happen before it actually did.

6

Putting Words in their Mouths

The entertainer Tommy Steele once announced that he was thinking of writing a novel. When he was asked what he thought would be the most difficult part, he replied, 'Finkin' of fings for the people to sye.'

I'm sure many new writers will sympathize with this. However, in fiction, we don't give our characters the power of speech to show off our talent for social intercourse. That's not dialogue. It's chat. And chat will kill your fiction like ivy smothering a rose.

New writers often balk at this. Chat, they reason, is part of life. It helps to add reality. Well, sure, life is full of chat. But why is it there? Mostly, to conceal the fact that we don't have anything more significant to say. Or if we do, the chat spins it out, like adding more potato when there's not enough meat.

This was brought vividly home to me when I bought a telephone-answering machine which could also record two-way conversations. Great, I thought, now when my partner is on the phone for three-quarters of an hour, I won't have to ask what the other person said. I'll be able to hear.

I only listened once – and I didn't last the distance. After the first few minutes I got so bored I switched off the tape.

It's the same for our readers. If they want a chat they can pick up the phone. If they've picked up a novel, they want the dialogue to *mean* something.

What's that stain on the carpet?

But what, precisely, is meaningful dialogue? Well, probably not this:

> Jill rang Sheila's doorbell.
>
> After a few moments, Sheila appeared, looking her usual harassed self. 'Hello, thought I heard the doorbell. I just made coffee. Want some?'
>
> 'That'd be nice, thanks.' Jill followed Sheila into the cheerful sitting room.
>
> 'Sit down, if you can find room. Sorry about the mess – I'm afraid Billy's just at that stage where he's into everything.'
>
> 'I know what it's like. When Kerry was two, she once tipped a whole bottle of tomato ketchup over the carpet. In the end, I had to hire one of those machines from the dry-cleaners.'
>
> Jill's voice floated from the hatch leading into the kitchen. 'What, you mean a steam-cleaner?'
>
> 'Oh, I don't know how they work, but it got most of the stuff out. I mean, if you look closely, there's still a bit of a stain . . .'

Mess – tomato ketchup – steam cleaners. Real life is full of such conversation, and in real life we'd accept it for what it is, a cosy bit of trivia. But not in fiction. In fiction, it's part of the unwritten contract between writer and reader that everything is there for a specific purpose. Consequently, any reader coming across the above passage would immediately wonder: Where are we heading here? What's the significance of the tomato ketchup? Am I suppose to *remember* that stain on the carpet?

And we, as writers, had better come up with something better than: I was trying to establish that the two of them are friends. Fine, says the reader, but can't you chew gum and walk at the same time? In other words, get on with the action, and blend the friendship with that.

What the reader really wants to know is: Why has Jill called round at Sheila's? Assuming there's a point to this scene, hint at it quickly. Everything else – friendship, tomato ketchup (if you must) and the names of their respective children (if important) can be woven in. Let's have another go:

Jill pressed Sheila's doorbell, keeping her finger there until she could see Sheila's dumpy figure through the frosted glass.

'Hey, Jill!' Sheila flung the door wide. 'I was hoping you'd drop by.'

You won't, thought Jill. Not when you've heard what I've got to say. She followed Sheila into the sitting room, skirting a bomb-site of Lego and numerous toy cars. 'Listen, Sheila—'

'Sorry about the mess.' Sheila scooped a pile of wooden pegs from the one decent armchair. 'I'm afraid Billy's into everything. I'll get some coffee.'

'No.' Jill put out a hand to stop her heading for the kitchen.

'What?' Sheila turned. Her eyes, wide and trusting, with those little gold flecks in them, were still for a moment. 'Why, sweetie, what on earth is it?'

Jill felt a pulse beating in her right temple. Don't chicken out now, she told herself. She has to know. And if you don't tell her, someone else will. 'Do you remember that day Kerry spilt tomato ketchup on our bedroom carpet?'

We don't have to know the significance of that tomato ketchup to see the difference between this and our first example. Here, the dialogue does double work. What Sheila says establishes the friendship. At the same time, what Jill says – and thinks – points to trouble ahead. So the reader's getting two messages at once. This gives the story a feeling of energy and *movement*.

All stories need movement. Without it, the effect is one of marching on the spot. Readers will only stand so much of that before asking: What's happening? Where's the entertainment?

In these terms, writers are illusionists and fictional dialogue is sleight of hand. However 'normal' it may appear, it is always a carefully crafted weave, in which every line has a purpose.

The main purposes of dialogue

Writers of How-to books are fond of listing the main purposes of dialogue. If you like memorizing lists, fine. If you don't, all you really need to remember is that every piece of dialogue must contribute to the momentum of the story. However, it may help you to remember that momentum is created when one or both of the following occurs:

1 The plot advances.

2 Interesting characters are illuminated.

In practice, it's difficult for a writer to interest a reader in characters until something happens to make them interesting. For this reason, most novels, certainly mass-market ones, use dialogue to get both plot and characters moving at the same time. The following extract from Stanley Ellin's *The Man from Nowhere* is an ingenious example of this principle in action:

The car was a gray coupé, a low-slung, high-powered brute, its rear seats piled high with luggage. When Jake swung it off the causeway in the direction of South Miami Beach the luggage shifted with a squeaking of expensive leather. He reached a hand behind him to shove it back into place.

He glanced at Elinor. 'How long have we been married?' he asked abruptly.

She came out of her daydream with a start and considered the question. 'Six months?'

'Wrong. If we were married on your birthday, which happens to be November tenth, and this is April fifth, it's not even five months yet. How long have we been married?'

'Not even five months yet.'

'Right. And during that five months certain little flaws in your character have come to light.'

'Naturally.'

'Do you know which one bugs me the most?'

'Yes, I talk too much. I'm too confiding. I tell our private business to anybody to comes along.'

'Why?'

'Look,' Elinor said, 'do we really have to go that deep into it?'

'We do.'

'All right then. Maybe it's because of you. I can't get through to you, so I talk my head off to anyone else who'll listen.'

This is no ordinary passage of dialogue. Let's see how it measures up against our two main purposes. Plot first. Something's cooking here. We know that because it's obvious from the disagreement over the wedding date that Jake and Elinor did not get married on November tenth. We know, too, that whatever they're pulling is important, because when Elinor protests Jake insists.

How about characterization? On the face of it, we're told

nothing, because the facts are sham. But it's clear that Jake is the one who's running the show. He's the one putting the questions, the one correcting, the one refusing to compromise. Note the word *abruptly* in his first line. They haven't been chatting before this. He's been absorbed in the plan, and she's been dreaming. Her tentative 'six months?' suggests that whatever's going down is washing over her head. She's involved, but can she be depended on?

In fact, Jake is a freelance insurance investigator and Elinor, hired for her beauty and sexual allure to help his cover in a stake-out, is a Greenwich Village ingenue. Her naivety is important because the author wants it to drive the plot forward in the later stages. So, plot and character are combined – and their first mix was in dialogue.

Note, too, that every line pays its way. There's no marching on the spot, while the writer allows the characters to make the same point twice. As a result, the piece moves. (If you want proof, try removing any line.)

The following extract from *The Old Devils* by Kingsley Amis shows another, rather different way of illuminating character. In this scene, Gwen and Malcolm Cellan-Davies have just learnt that a couple from their past, Alun and Rhiannon Weaver, are returning to live in Wales:

'It'll be, er, fun seeing Rhiannon again,' she said.

'M'm.'

'Been a long time, hasn't it? What, ten years?'

'At least that. More like fifteen.'

'She never came down with Alun on any of his trips after whenever it was. Just once, or twice was it?'

'She used to come down to see her mother at Broughton, and then the old girl died about that long ago, so she probably . . .'

'I dare say you'd remember. I just thought it was funny she never really kept up with her college friends or anyone else as far as I know.'

Malcolm said nothing to that. He swayed from side to side in his chair as a way of suggesting that life held many such small puzzles.

'Well, she'll have plenty of time from now on, or rather from next month. I hope she doesn't find it too slow for her in these parts after London.'

'A lot of people she knew will still be here.'

'That's the whole trouble,' said Gwen, laughing slightly.

What Amis has done here is clever. In terms of factual information, the dialogue illuminates Rhiannon Weaver: it's ten or fifteen years since she was in Wales, her mother died, she lost touch with her friends, she lives in London, but now she's returning. That last detail is a plotting signpost. It shows us where we're headed.

But the function of this dialogue doesn't stop there. Instead, from Gwen's first provocative comment, 'It'll be, er, fun seeing Rhiannon again,' we can see that this is a multi-purpose passage with meaningful undercurrents. Malcolm's lines, his throwaway 'M'm', swiftly followed by his recall of detail, reveal rather more about him and his feelings for Rhiannon. As a result we start to ponder the nature of their relationship. This involves us with the characters. Finally, Gwen's oblique 'That's the whole trouble', followed by her 'slight' laugh switch us back to plot and the conflict ahead.

So, let's summarize exactly what the dialogue achieves here. It:

1 Gives direction to the plot. We know now that something is likely to happen when Rhiannon arrives.
2 Illuminates Rhiannon, in advance of her appearance, stimulating our interest in her.
3 Illuminates Malcolm.
4 Illuminates Gwen.
5 Provokes reader speculation about several relationships.

It's the combination of purposes that makes this passage so powerful. Don't fret if your own dialogue isn't quite so concentrated. This novel won the Booker Prize. It's supposed to be good.

However, it's always useful to compare your own work with that of the masters. If it's consistently 'thinner' and less purposeful, try reworking it. The best test of all is that of necessity. If a line doesn't add anything significant, it shouldn't be there. You may find it helpful to think of dialogue as a tennis match, in which the ball must keep moving, causing the players to react.

We'll be talking more about the possibilities of dialogue in Chapters Seven and Eight. But now, let's look at an alternative to dialogue and why you might want to use it.

Dialogue or summary narrative?

As you work through your novel, there'll be many occasions on which you must decide whether to write dialogue in full, or to summarize it. Suppose, for example, that two friends are arranging to meet. The actual conversation may go something like this:

Jenny: How about Thursday?
Gail: No, that's my badminton night. Friday'd be better.
Jenny: Can't make Friday. It'll have to be Monday.
Gail: OK, shall we say seven?
Jenny: Better make it eight. Oh, no, wait, I promised to...

Theoretically, this could go on for half a page. Real it may be, but it's going nowhere. Unless there's some ulterior significance to these lines, scrap them for summary narrative: 'After checking their diaries, they made a date for Tuesday at eight-thirty.'

Summary narrative is also the perfect solution for all

those social niceties: goodbyes, hellos, introductions and telephone small talk:

The phone rang. *It was Graham, wanting to know if I'd seen Jem.*

'I thought he was with you,' I said, and then I started to worry.

Here, the summary narrative (in italics) allows you to skip the boring bits and cut to what matters. Imagine two people are having an argument. It's a real humdinger, and the insults are flying. Don't be tempted to record it all faithfully, based on the reasoning that quarrels are conflict, and the readers like conflict. Even conflict must have a goal, a direction, or it's nothing more than a loud noise.

The answer is to condense the quarrel, replacing some of the dialogue with indirect discourse:

'And another thing,' she said, 'I don't like it when you're late home. I've got your dinner in the oven, and you don't even show? What kind of consideration is that, huh?'

She didn't want an answer. She'd got good and angry and now she wanted to row. I let her rip for about ten minutes, then when she started to cry, I took her in my arms and told her I loved her.

'You don't love me.' She was still angry, but she didn't struggle.

'Of course I do,' I said. 'Why d'you think I work so hard? It's to earn more money for us. Surely you understand that?'

Here, that second paragraph lets us know what's happening without clogging up the works with superfluous information.

Think of using summary narrative whenever a character is talking a lot without moving the story forward – explaining something at length, recalling the past, indulging in anecdotes which aren't part of the plot. The following passage is a good example:

> He stayed past midnight, telling them about miraculous escapes from predatory animals, the constant pain of hunger, and a vision of Marilyn Monroe dispensing chocolate chip cookies to the ones who had died.

Here summary narrative gives us the picture without boring the reader with unnecessary detail.

One word of warning: summary narrative does not have the same immediacy or credibility as straight dialogue. That's why it's good for trivia, bad for impact. Always use dialogue for the big moments, the crucial lines:

> After dinner, they chatted for a while about their respective days. She told him about the blocked drain and how the milkman had left semi-skimmed instead of full cream. He told her about the traffic on the bypass. And then, finally, when she got up to fetch the coffee, he came right out with it.
>
> 'Amy,' he said. 'I've been given the push.'

How do we write it?

If dialogue is to be effective it must be presented in such a way that it's effortless to read. Your guide here is: think of the readers. Dialogue that makes them hesitate – even for a moment, to wonder, 'Who's speaking here?' or 'Did I read this right?' needs fixing fast.

Dialogue has conventions. You probably know them, but I'll spin through them anyway, using this extract from *City Primeval*, by Elmore Leonard:

> 'I think you're afraid of women,' the girl from the *News* said. 'I think that's the root of the problem.'
>
> Raymond Cruz wasn't sure whose problem she was referring to, if it was supposed to be his problem or hers [1].
>
> She said [2], 'Do you think women are devious?'

'You mean women reporters?'

'Women in general.'

Sitting in Carl's Chop House surrounded by an expanse of empty white tablecloths, their waitress off somewhere, Raymond Cruz wondered if it was worth the free drinks and dinner or the effort required to give thoughtful answers.

'No,' he said [3].

'You don't feel intimidated by women?'

'No, I've always liked women.'

'At certain times,' the girl from the *News* said. 'Otherwise, I'd say you're indifferent to women. They don't fit into your male world.'

Let's see what we can learn from this. First, look at the arrangement of the paragraphs. There's a new one for each change of speaker and also for the switches from speaker to observer and vice versa. Take a look at [1]. Even though Raymond says nothing in this paragraph, and many new writers might be tempted to let the previous paragraph run on, this would be a mistake. New paragraphs alert the reader to change in a way that run-ons don't.

[2] Why has the writer put the tag 'She said' before, instead of after, the speech? To avoid confusion. There's a rather peculiar convention in fiction that the last person mentioned is the next one to speak (unless it's specifically made clear that the character says nothing). For example, it's not a good idea to write something like this:

'Raymond was irritated.

' "I think you're playing a role. What're you afraid of?" the girl from the *News* said.'

What's wrong with that? Because Raymond was the last person mentioned, readers will assume that he's the one speaking – yes, even with the new paragraph. The speech tag corrects this, but it's too late. The reader has to make a readjustment and readjustments, however trivial, are disruptive.

[3] This proves the previous point. There's no speech tag in front of the 'No', but I bet you knew who was speaking.

Now, look again at [3]. Since the previous paragraph details Raymond's action, why do we need a new paragraph when he starts to speak? The answer is that we don't. It would be perfectly acceptable if the author had written:

'Raymond Cruz wondered if it was worth the free drinks and dinner or the effort required to give thoughtful answers. "No," he said.'

In choosing to split that paragraph in two, Leonard implies a pause between Raymond's thought and his 'No'. As such, I think it works better, but it's a matter of personal judgement.

Similarly, if a character's dialogue is *followed* by a thought or action, you can choose to write it like this:

"No," Raymond said. He picked up his beer, drained the glass, and watched her light another cigarette.'

Or like this:

'"No," said Raymond.

'He picked up his beer, drained the glass, and watched her light another cigarette.'

In this instance, I'd probably go for the former, but if the second paragraph were longer I might change my mind. Never worry about your paragraphs being too short. Short paragraphs devour space and look good on the page. This is particularly important in genre fiction, including category romance. Barbara Cartland (and she should know) never writes paragraphs more than three lines long. She claims this makes her books look like conversation. 'They are easy to read, and once people have started they go on reading them.'

A word about quotation marks. Some writers, notably Irish ones, don't use quotes for their dialogue:

Jimmy was going to see if he could recruit Declan Cuffe.
He took his tray and went over to where he was sitting.

> – Sorry, eh – Declan, said Jimmy. – Is there anyone sittin' here?
> Declan Cuffe leaned over the table and studied the chair.
> Then he said: – It doesn't look like it.

This is from *The Commitments* by Roddy Doyle, a book written almost entirely in dialogue. The speech marks are dashes –, a technique employed by James Joyce. One critic has suggested that this shows the characters breaking into speech rather than hanging up their speech marks to say, 'Please may I speak now?' An intriguing idea, but one which some people – readers, this time – have found awkward and intrusive. If you can write like Roddy Doyle, you may get away with it. If not – well, I'll leave that with you.

Speech tags

Many writers get themselves in a stew over speech tags. Is it OK to use 'he said', 'she said' all the time? Is it bad to use elegant variations such as 'he expostulated' or 'she breathed'? What about adverbs: 'she argued hotly', 'he answered brutally'?

The truth is that there is no absolute rule. It depends on the kind of book you're writing, the intended readership, and the effect you want to achieve. As a rough guide – and I do mean rough – the more literary the novel, the plainer the speech tags. Some writers make it a rule never to use anything other than *said*. This will certainly keep you out of trouble, and there's no need to worry about sounding repetitious. Unlike elegant variation, plain *said* blends into text like invisible ink.

In *The French Lieutenant's Woman*, John Fowles has dispensed with speech tags altogether:

> It was only then that he noticed, or at least realized the sex of, the figure at the end.

'Good heavens, I took that to be a fisherman. But isn't it a woman?'

Ernestina peered – her grey, her very pretty eyes, were short-sighted, and all she could see was a dark shape.

'Is she young?'

'It's too far to tell.'

'But I can guess who it is. It must be poor Tragedy.'

'Tragedy?'

'A nickname. One of her nicknames.'

'And what are the others?'

Theoretically, good dialogue can stand alone. The danger is that without any speech tags it's easy to get confused. You only have to glance up from the page and you don't know who's speaking.

By the way, I hope you noticed that not only has Fowles split action and speech into separate paragraphs, but he's also taken advantage of the last-person-mentioned-is-first-one-to-speak convention?

Now, take a look at this:

Sara shook her head. 'You mean your father doesn't approve of Jude?' she ventured, forced to make some comment, and Venetia grimaced.

'He wants me to marry someone with lots of money and a title,' she exclaimed bitterly. 'He won't listen to what I want.'

Sara's fingers tightened on the wheel. 'I'm sure your father knows best,' she observed, and Venetia snorted.

'I suppose I should have expected that,' she muttered.

No prizes for guessing that this is not a literary novel. It's a Mills & Boon romance (*Duelling Fire* by Anne Mather) and the dialogue style is distinctive. Here, the characters don't merely speak. They 'venture', 'exclaim bitterly', 'observe' or 'mutter'. There's a reason for this. Varied speech tags inject a feeling of activity. It may be sham but it works. (Try replacing those variations with 'she said' and see the effect.)

Charlotte Lamb, whose light romances have sold fifty million copies, says that Mills & Boon prefer explicit writing because the readers are interested in action, not interpretation. They want everything mirror-clear: how the heroine speaks or the hero replies. For this reason, adverbs are important. If you leave them out, the publishers will ask you to put them back in.

Does this mean that, if we're not writing a romance, we shouldn't use adverbs or speech tag variations? Well, no. But I think it pays to recognize the difference between spurious and functional variation. Words like 'answered', 'commented' or 'echoed' don't really add anything to the writing. But there's a big difference between '"Open the door," she said softly,' and '"Open the door," she yelled.'

You might have noticed something else about the last passage. Each speech is accompanied by a gesture showing the character's response: a shake of the head, a grimace, a tightening of fingers. This heightens the feeling of movement, and gives the scene an almost filmic quality. In the TV age, this is important. It's a useful technique. Graham Greene used it to back up plain speech tags. For example, 'He said with his habitual gritty grin.'

Finally, you could try Raymond Chandler's technique of adding a touch of sensory detail:

- 'How do you feel?' It was a smooth silvery voice that matched her hair.

- 'What's the matter, honey?' He had a solid blurring voice, with just the right sappy tone to belong to a guy who would go for a woman with gilded toenails.

- 'You have said what?' she got out at last, in a voice as silky as burnt toast.

7

Cool Things to do with Dialogue

Dialogue is a little like an expensive camera or the latest VCR. It has a lot of buttons, which many people ignore because they don't know how they work. This is a pity because dialogue can perform all sorts of clever tricks, which – once you know how to use them – will give your writing extra power. In the last chapter, we talked a bit about multi-purpose dialogue. Let's now have a closer look at some of dialogue's special features and what they can do for you.

Dialogue as a short-cut

A short-cut gets you to where you want to go, only faster. Suppose you have a main character who had a rotten childhood. His father beat him and his mother was an alcoholic; neither of them had dinner ready when he came home from school. Unloved and miserable, he starts to roam the streets and eventually turns to a life of crime. Years later, in jail, the prison psychologist asks him: 'What was your childhood like?'

If your story starts here, how are you going to handle that deprived background? How are you going to get the information across? You have several options. Using straight dialogue, you could simply allow your character to tell his tale. This would take up a lot of space and, because it's exposition and not action, it will effectively stop the forward movement of the story.

You could put in a flashback, showing the character's former life. Technically, this too will stop the story, but because flashbacks are scenic the reader gets a sense of drama – even though it's past.

Or you could do something else.

In the film *Escape from Alcatraz*, a prison psychologist put this very question, 'What was your childhood like?', to the character played by Clint Eastwood. The reply: 'Short.'

That single word is a pearl of short-cut dialogue. It speaks volumes, not just about the character's past, but about his frame of mind now. Best of all it doesn't hold up the action for a chunk of explanation. It allows the plot to move forward instead of putting down roots.

In real life, talk is free. In fiction, it costs money. If we expect readers to shell out their hard-earned cash for our fantasies, the least we can do is to give them good value. Richard Walter, whose screenwriting classes at the University of California have helped hundreds of writers become successful professionals, puts it more succinctly: 'Dialogue has to be worth waiting in line for. Unless it writhes and wriggles, glows and glistens, it is unworthy of any audience.'

Although he's talking about movies, the same principle applies in novels. Film is a good medium to study for dialogue because you know that every line has been pruned and polished to the director's satisfaction. It will fulfil its purpose as fast and economically as its writer knows how.

If you want to write great short-cut dialogue, here's an exercise you can do next time you watch a video.

An exercise in dialogue

Take any scene and write down the dialogue, just as it's spoken. Try to include the whole scene if you can, because films can teach you a lot about starting and finishing. Then use the dialogue to write up that scene as it might appear in a novel, adding descriptive detail, facial expressions, action and so on as you remember it from the film. If you're feeling adventurous, you might also try adding what doesn't appear: the main character's thoughts.

I promise you that the mental activity involved in putting the dialogue into a visual context, in choosing the right words to convey the various characters' reactions, will teach you a lot, not just about the power of snappy dialogue, but about writing in general. Because the film exists in picture form in your head, it will show you what your own stories should 'look' like before you get them down on paper. And, by learning to visualize your own scenes, you'll add a clarity that's sadly missing from many writers' first novels.

As a teenager, long before VCRs were invented, I used to write down dialogue in the cinema so as to record my favourite films in text form. In those days, films were usually book adaptations, but more often than not the books were so unlike their screen counterparts as to be unrecognizable. To avoid disappointment, I wrote my own version. Nowadays, many authors earn a good living writing the book of the film, and there's no need to do it yourself. I'm glad I did because when I started writing fiction, dialogue came naturally. It will for you too, if you practise this exercise.

Verbal irony in dialogue

Voltaire said that we use words only to conceal our thoughts. There's some truth in this. Certainly, real people don't like being too up-front about themselves. I don't think, for example, that too many of us would stand up in public and say: 'Hello, folks, I'm a lazy, selfish person whose ambition is to win the pools and go and live in Barbados with Sharon Stone/Harrison Ford.'

Consequently, if fictional characters are too open about themselves, readers will feel as if the writer's spoon-feeding them. The story will fail to hold attention because there's nothing for the reader to do.

One way for us to cope with this, and still project our characters, is to use verbal irony. Irony comes in many forms, but verbal irony occurs when the reader is aware that there's a 'gap', or contrast, between what's said and what's meant. For example, if a man tells a woman he loves her while glancing at his watch, we're pretty safe in assuming he's lying. Similarly, if a character has been seen breaking a promise earlier in the book, we know that when he says, 'Trust me, I won't tell a soul,' he probably doesn't mean it.

Verbal irony must be set up. If the reader misses it and takes the dialogue at face value, the point will be lost. Take a look at this passage from David Lodge's *Nice Work*, in which viewpoint character Vic Wilcox (he of the coloured lavatories) is talking to Brian, his marketing director. Brian arrives late for work, complaining of contraflow hold-ups.

> 'You should live in the city, like me, Brian. Not thirty miles away.'
>
> 'Oh, you know what Beryl is like,' says Brian Everthorpe, with a smile designed to be rueful.
>
> Vic doesn't know. He has never met Beryl, said to be Everthorpe's second wife, and formerly his secretary. As far as he knows, Beryl may not even exist, except as an excuse for Brian Everthorpe's delinquencies. Beryl says the kids need country air. Beryl was poorly this morning and I had to run her to the doctor's. Beryl sends her apologies – she forgot to give me your message. One day, quite soon in fact,

Brian Everthorpe is going to have to concentrate his mind
on the differences between a wife and an employer.

In this scene, we meet Brian Everthorpe for the first time,
and he's making an excuse. It may well be genuine, but we
suspect not. Why? Because the author has given us Vic's
thoughts as a contrast, and Vic has already been established
as a shrewd bloke. Vic knows no more of what's going on in
Brian's mind than we do. However, he does recollect a string
of previous excuses, the similarity of which suggests that
Brian may well be what Vic thinks he is: an irresponsible
layabout. We are now alerted to future contradictions
between Brian's speech and actions. This stimulates our
interest whenever he appears.

Dialogue as springboard

I'm sure we've all read books that were so exciting we
simply couldn't put them down. One way to achieve this is
to let the dialogue springboard the reader into the next
chapter. Here, for example, is the end of one chapter from
The Twisted Window, a young adult suspense novel by Lois
Duncan:

> I don't want to get involved in this, thought Tracey. I don't
> want my life touched by anybody else's. I don't want to care
> about Mindy, I don't want to care about Brad – I don't want
> to invest myself in anyone again.
>
> Considering the situation though, she knew she had no
> alternative.
>
> 'What exactly do you want me to do?' she asked.

Only the most incurious – or extremely thirsty reader –
would fail to turn the page here. Romantic novels often
employ this technique. The reader, who has a natural dislike
of unfinished business, thinks, 'Oh, I'll just look at the next

bit before I put out the light,' and before she knows it, she's read the whole book.

Dialogue as suspense

Sometimes, it's not what characters say that's important but what they leave unsaid. Leaving the reader's imagination to fill in the gap can be highly effective, particularly in thrillers, where it adds to the suspense. In this scene from Barbara Vine's *A Fatal Inversion*, two characters dig a grave for their dog:

> He plunged the spade in once more, slicing into the firm, dry turf. As he did so he saw that Meg was holding out her spade to him. On it lay what looked like the bones, the fan splay of metatarsals, of a very small foot.
>
> 'A monkey?' Meg said in a faint faltering voice.
>
> 'It must be.'
>
> 'Why hasn't it got a headstone?'
>
> He didn't answer. He dug down, lifting out spade-loads of resin-scented earth. Meg was digging up bones, she had a pile of them.
>
> 'We'll put them in a box or something. We'll re-bury them.'
>
> 'No,' he said. 'No, we can't do that. Meg...?'
>
> 'What is it? What's the matter?'
>
> 'Look,' he said, and he lifted it up to show her. 'That's not a dog's skull, is it? That's not a monkey's?'

The scene ends there, with the author resisting the temptation to let the dialogue run on. The effect of this is to stimulate the readers' imagination, to make them the possessors of the unspeakable – which is that much more suspenseful that if you spelt it all out.

Dialogue as pacing

Pacing means the speed at which a story progresses. Stories slow down when the action stops. And once a story slows down, there's always a danger of losing the reader. The prime example of a pacing problem occurs in those old murder mysteries where the detective summons the suspects and launches into a wodge of explanatory tedium, pausing only to cough momentously and adjust his cravat.

Chances are that sooner or later you too will be the proud owner of explanatory dialogue. How do you deal with it? Well, Dean Koontz encountered this problem near the end of his horror novel, *The Bad Place*. He solved it by splicing together two different dialogues. In the following scene, Bobby Dakota is the captive audience of Doc Fogarty, whose role is to reveal the horrible secrets of Candy Pollard, a killer on the trail of Bobby and his wife. It's the kind of question-and-answer session which – because it lasts for some twenty pages – could lose its impact if delivered in a lump:

> Bobby knew he had to remain sober and he was aware of the danger of too much bourbon after a night of too little sleep. But he had a hunch that he was burning it off as fast as he drank it, at least for now. He took another sip before he said, 'You're not telling us that beefy hulk is hermaphroditic too?'
>
> 'Oh, no,' Fogarty said. 'Worse than that.'

At this tantalizing point, the author cuts and runs to a different dialogue between the 'beefy hulk', Candy, and his clairvoyant sister, Violet:

> Candy opened the door. 'What do you want?'
>
> 'He's here, in town right now,' she said.
>
> His eyes widened.
>
> 'You mean Frank?'
>
> 'Yes.'

Now the reader's intense curiosity about Candy's deviations is overlaid by fear for Bobby's safety. You see, Frank is with Bobby, and Candy wants both of them. We know it's only a matter of time before Violet 'sees' their exact location. Then Candy will move and they won't know what hit them. Koontz now switches deftly back to Doc Fogarty, who is calmly explaining that Candy has four testicles but no penis:

> ' "To put it in layman's language: this guy is seriously stoked with sexual tension that he can't possibly release, he's rechanneled that energy into other outlets, mainly acts of incredible violence, and he's as dangerous as any monster any moviemaker ever dreamed up." '

See how the pace, instead of flagging, has gone up a notch? 'STOP TALKING!' the reader wants to scream. 'Get out now before it's too late!'

You don't have to wait until you have an explanatory wodge before trying this technique. You can use dialogue to break up or pace any action that's happening simultaneously. For example, suppose you have a character who's been kidnapped and held in a deserted farmhouse. You can effectively switch from dialogue between the victim and his kidnapper to dialogue between the people trying to find him.

Alternatively, if the victim is alone, the dialogue between his rescuers will add movement and variety. Similarly, use dialogue to speed up any slow-moving narrative. Why not experiment right now? Use dialogue to pace the following twin scenarios, or use your own ideas:

- A hitman making his final preparations while the victim and his wife are having a row.

- A host and hostess discussing the imminent arrival of guests while the guests are talking about the host and hostess.

- A wife confessing her adultery to her husband while her lover is unfaithful with another woman.

- Fugitives fleeing from the law while the law is closing in.

Note: Don't cut and splice gratuitously throughout a whole book. If you're not sure why, reread Chapter Three.

Dialogue as chat

As we saw in the last chapter, chat has no place in fiction. But take a look at this passage from Kingsley Amis's *Ending Up*.

'What's your news, Goldie?' asked Trevor, using the diminutive Marigold had decreed upon her grandchildren.

'You don't want to listen to an old woman's gossip.'

'Just who you've heard from, that sort of thing,' said Trevor with commendable speed.

'Now, which of my chummy-wummies would you remember? ... What about Jill Grigson-Morse? She used to come to us in Beauchamp Place.'

Trevor's face seemed to light up. 'Oh, yes.'

'No, you couldn't have seen her there, because she didn't come back from Italy until after we'd left Beauchamp Place. Her husband had a job in the Diplomatic, I think, or ...'

'How's he getting on?'

'Oh, he died, it must be ten years ago. A very slow and painful cancer. She was absolutely marvellous all the way to the end. She's a brave woman.'

'How is she these days?'

'I was just coming to that. I had a letter from her yesterday or the day before. They've had to take her other leg off, but she's awfully good about it. I do so admire people like that.'

Here we have a seventy-three-old woman ostensibly chatting with her grandson but in reality laying herself bare. Let's look at the features. First, her reference to 'chummy-wummies' is a character tag. Earlier, the reader learns that Marigold once had a 'checkle-peckle' returned by her bank because it had been made out for five 'poundies'. This shows a woman clinging – albeit unconsciously – to the language of her youth.

Secondly, we can see, or rather hear, that her mind is not as clear as it might be. Although she appears perfectly clear about the time Jill came back from Italy, she can't remember whether Jill's husband was a diplomat. Similarly, she doesn't know whether a letter arrived yesterday or the day before.

At this point in the story, we don't know how Marigold feels about this – or even if she's aware of it. However, we can't help noticing her faintly glib references to death and suffering. Her description of Jill as 'marvellous' and 'awfully good' about losing her leg suggests that Marigold is absolutely determined not to let life drag her down. Later, when we find out that she has noticed her little lapses, it comes as no surprise that what she dreads most is turning into a vegetable.

It's not always easy to disguise significant detail as chat, but it's well worth trying because it does give our work the illusion of reality.

I've no doubt that some enterprising psychotherapist will one day write a book about the hidden meanings in trivial conversation – which will, of couse, be an instant best-seller. Until then, why not try your own little experiment? Next time you're talking to someone you don't know very well, see what you can learn about them from the content of their chat. You may be surprised. For example, even a banal comment on the weather: 'It'll be raining tomorrow, you mark my words' identifies the speaker as a pessimist. An optimist would say, 'Lovely day. Let's hope it keeps up.'

Here's a little tip Alan Whicker once revealed in a TV interview. When you're listening to someone and they stop talking, don't rush to fill in the silence – however much you're tempted. Just wait and look interested. Most people find silences uncomfortable and, if you hold out, they'll be forced to speak. What they say will be more revealing because they haven't prepared it, or had time to run it past their internal censor.

Another use of 'chat' is as a smokescreen. In real life, we often use chat to disguise strong emotions like grief, anger, love or embarrassment. In the film *Annie Hall*, there's a scene between Woody Allen and Diane Keaton in which the dialogue is totally trivial and banal. What makes it amusing is the addition of voiceovers which tell us what the characters are thinking.

On film, this is an unusual technique. In a novel, we can reveal thought any time we want. If that thought contrasts with what a character is saying, the reader feels involved – and I probably don't need to remind you that's no bad thing.

Student Example

The phone rang. 'Pamela? It's me.'

'Oh, hi,' I said. Why does she *never* give her name when I answer? It's as if she imagines she's the only one who phones me.

'Sorry to call so early. I hope it isn't inconvenient.'

'No, not at all.' Of course it's inconvenient! It's eight in the morning, I'm in the middle to getting the children's breakfast, I've still got to shower, and we've all got to leave by eight thirty.

'Pamela, I need a really *big* favour. Please say you'll help.'

'Well, I will if I can.' Hurry up, just say what you want. I haven't got all day.

'Oh, great! You remember I bought some curtains for my spare room, the white ones with yellow roses?'

Well, I wouldn't have chosen them. The yellow was far too acid to go with the wallpaper. 'Yes, they were really nice.'

'Well, Richard's mother has just announced she's arriving tomorrow and the curtains are too short.'

'Oh, dear.' Didn't you measure the window, you stupid woman?

'Could you change them for me in your lunch hour? I've got so much to do before Ma-in-law arrives.'

'Today? Do you mean today?' Oh, please God don't let it be today. I'm only taking half an hour's break so I can leave early.

'Yes, please. It's got to be today so I can hang them before she arrives.'

'Well, I suppose I can.' It'll mean I don't get to eat lunch, but what the hell, that doesn't matter so long as you impress your mother-in-law. And why can't you get into town? You're so selfish! I work. You don't.

'Great, thanks. I owe you one.'

'That's OK. I don't mind.' Yes, I do, I mind like hell.

'I'll have the curtains ready for you to pick up after you've dropped the kids off at school.'

'Could you bring them round to me? I'm running a little late.' I'm *very* late and I'll be even later if I have to stop at your house.

'Ooh, it would be much better for me if you called here. I'm not dressed yet.'

'Uh – well, OK, but I can't stop. I've got to get to work.' And you haven't and now I'm in a foul mood and I'll shout at the children and arrive at work and have to apologise for being late and I should have said no right at the beginning.

'Bye then, see you soon.'
'Bye.' Damn, damn, damn.

Judy Smith

Dialogue as tension

Someone once said that the word 'No' is essential in fiction because it establishes contending forces. True, but it's not the word itself that's important; it's the tension it generates. Tension is the essence of all drama because it creates that vital feeling of movement. Even at the simplest level, a scene in which two characters cannot agree is always more stimulating than one in which they're saying: 'Oh, yeah, you're so right,' or 'Couldn't have put it better myself.' (If you're at all unsure about this, you've obviously never been in a restaurant where someone's having an argument.)

The effect of characters at odds is twofold. Firstly, the reader will be tempted to take sides. This is a great way to forge a bond between reader and character. Secondly, the reader will want to know the outcome. When characters agree, the readers' questions are resolved. Result: end of story.

But tension can be subtle, too. A very effective technique is to put your characters in different states of mind. We all know, for example, how tension-generating it is to have someone bounce into the room when we're feeling depressed, saying: 'C'mon, the sun's shining, it's a great day; pull yourself together!' Or to be excited when someone else is calm. Or to be drunk and giggly when someone else is bootfacedly sober.

Readers, too, will feel a ripple of tension whenever you offer them a similar mismatch of emotion or attitude. This is where the character contrasts we discussed in Chapter Four will start to pay dividends. Your characters can now reveal those contrasts in their dialogue with others.

In the following passage from E. M. Forster's *A Room With a View*, the attitude of the prudish and socially aware Miss Bartlett contrasts sharply with the more open and – in Miss Bartlett's opinion – ill-bred Mr Emerson. The scene is dinner at a Florentine guesthouse. Miss Bartlett is determined to reject Mr Emerson's offer of a room with a view:

'This is my son,' said the old man; 'his name's George. He has a view, too.'

'Ah,' said Miss Bartlett, repressing Lucy, who was about to speak.

'What I mean,' he continued, 'is that you can have our rooms, we'll have yours. We'll change.'

The better class of tourist was shocked at this, and sympathized with the newcomers. Miss Bartlett, in reply, opened her mouth as little as possible and said:

'Thank you very much indeed; that is out of the question.'

'Why?' said the old man, with both fists on the table.

'Because it is quite out of the question, thank you.'

'You see, we don't like to take—' began Lucy.

Her cousin again repressed her.

'But why?' he persisted. 'Women like looking at a view; men don't.' And he thumped with his fists like a naughty child and turned to his son, saying, 'George, persuade them!'

'It's so obvious they should have the rooms,' said the son. 'There's nothing else to say.'

This being a novel, there's plenty more to say. And the readers will listen because what this passage does so beautifully is to stimulate interest in the various characters.

Let dialogue take a break

Finally, a useful lesson for any writer to learn is when *not* to use dialogue. Suppose a person discovers that their lover/spouse is having an affair. Dialogue is one way of handling this. We're all familiar with the telephone conversation that just happens to be overhead, or the door that just happens to be ajar while the lovers are talking. But sometimes action can substitute for dialogue and be far more effective.

In *The Birds of the Air*, Alice Thomas Ellis lets her character, Barbara, throw a pre-Christmas party:

> At last she reached the bookcase in the other room, where she had hidden the after-dinner mints away from Sam. She was just in time to see her husband placing a piece of turkey with his fork in the damp red mouth of the Professor of Music, whose own hands were taken up with her glass and her embroidered ethnic evening handbag, hung with tassels and studded with bits of mirror.
>
> This playful, lascivious act was so uncharacteristic of Sebastian, and suited him so ill, that for a moment Barbara failed to recognise him. She felt suddenly deathly faint, and then she realised for herself what Sam had learnt at tea time and what everyone else had known for months.

An even more subtle unmasking occurs in *The Tall Guy*, a film in which the heroine sees her boyfriend hand a drink to a woman who doesn't say 'Thank you'. As the heroine points out, you have to know someone *really* well not to say thank you in social situations. The audience, by the way, is already aware that the hero is being unfaithful. They are waiting for him to betray himself, but they don't expect it to happen like this.

If you can similarly surprise your reader, that's all to the good.

8

How to Write More Convincing Dialogue

Many writers have problems with dialogue because they forget what it is: an individualized expression of characters' thoughts, feelings and intellect. True, in fiction, one of dialogue's prime purposes is to advance the plot, but it must never be allowed to turn the characters into glove puppets. When the writer forgets this, the dialogue loses flavour and descends into what's probably best described as the flat-pack-wardrobe style of writing:

'Look,' said Linda, pointing at a road, half-hidden by over-hanging trees. 'That must be the lane that leads to the castle.'

'Well-spotted,' said Alan, slamming his foot on the brake. 'And if I'm not mistaken, someone's been here before us. Just look at those tyre-marks.'

'And that someone obviously didn't intend us to follow them.' Linda's well-manicured hand flew to her mouth. 'Watch out, there's an enormous log in the middle of the road!'

I'm not going to insult you by pointing out what's wrong with that particular passage. Instead, I'm going to offer you a three-step guide to writing dialogue that sounds natural, is right for your characters, and reads like a dream. What more can you ask?

Great dialogue in three easy steps

Step One: hearing voices

If we want to produce the kind of dialogue that's 'worth waiting in line for', we must first hear it in our heads like the real thing. If you've never heard voices in your head you may well feel that this is the first step to a straitjacket and a white van.

Relax. 'As a writer one is allowed to have conversations with oneself. What is considered sane in writers is mad for the rest of the human race.' Alan Ayckbourn said that and I think most novelists would agree with him. Josephine Hart claims that both her novels *Damage* and *Sin*, were 'conceived and nurtured as I raced around London, head down, lost in imaginary conversations with my characters, and indeed so overwhelmed by their emotions that I would find myself weeping in the street'.

The key to forging such a bond with your characters is creative visualization. If you don't like the idea of weeping in the street, and I can't say I fancy the idea myself, try the following visualization in the comfort of your own writer's retreat, the place you created in Chapter One. This visualization will generate the kind of emotional atmosphere in which voices should come naturally.

Visualization One: unfinished business You're in your retreat. You're feeling calm. Nothing can threaten you. The air is pleasantly warm on your skin. Somewhere in the distance, you can hear water, the trickle of a stream, or perhaps a fountain. Take a few deep breaths and think back to one of those times in your life when you wanted to say something, but didn't. Maybe the other person wasn't listening. Maybe you were embarrassed or scared of making a fool of yourself. Maybe you were just scared. Or maybe you just couldn't think of the right words to use. Now's your chance.

It doesn't matter who the other person is. It could be: a teacher you always hated; a lover who betrayed you, or one you betrayed; a friend; an enemy; your ex-wife; your mother; your father.

In your imagination, decide on a place in which you will feel comfortable meeting and talking to this person. Remember, he or she comes to you by invitation only. Nothing can hurt you in any way.

In your mind, see yourself sitting down with this person in the setting you have chosen. Start to bring up all your senses, one by one. What clothes is the person wearing? Notice texture and colour. Be aware of any scent or smell. Be aware, too, of your own sensations, the saliva in your mouth, the sound of your breathing, the feel of your throat.

When you're ready, look into this person's eyes, and say your piece. Hear your voice as you speak, the words, the intonation, the pauses in between.

Now let the person reply to you in his or her own voice. Listen to this voice as carefully as you did to your own. Be aware of how you feel. This is important because fiction is about action and reaction. When one of your characters speaks, you need to know what he or she is feeling.

Feel free to continue this dialogue for as long as you want. Remember, this is a fantasy. You can say anything you want, and anything can happen, but it's all quite safe. When you're finished, return to your retreat and spend a few moments alone.

Note: If you have any problems with this visualization, try

doing it in a deep warm bath when you're feeling tired. In my experience at writers' workshops, even the most reluctant visualizers find themselves having fantasies while lying in the bath.

Step Two: liaise with your cast

In fiction, there's no way we can convey the precise sound of a character's voice. Even imagery – 'Her voice is like gravel spread with honey' (from Jay McInerney's *Bright Lights, Big City*) – will evoke a different sound for different readers. This doesn't matter. What's important is that we, the writers, must be familiar with the voice. Even more vital, the voice must be the character's own, distinct both from other characters' and also from the author's. I'm talking here not about accent or dialect, but about the kind of elusive singularity we also see in faces, making every one unique. Without this uniqueness, the character is little more than his creator's mouthpiece.

John Mortimer talks about 'the magical moment when a character has come so completely to life that he or she will do something quite unexpected, something the author had never intended and which sends the story off into new and uncharted territory.' This is great – if it works. However, there's a fine line between setting our characters free to be themselves and allowing them to grab the wheel and burn rubber.

In my experience, there's only one way to tread this fine line. We must meet our characters and let them talk freely. The American writer Gore Vidal said: 'Each writer is born with a repertory company in his head and ... as you get older, you become more skilful in casting them.' The next visualization is designed to help you do this.

Visualization Two: the empire speaks back Spend a few minutes getting relaxed in your retreat. After a while, when you feel comfortable, look around you. To your right, there's a door. You may not have noticed this door before, but it's a very special one. From now on, whenever you want to get in touch with your characters, all you have to do is to open this door.

Try opening it now. See the stone steps leading down to a river. Willow trees fringe the river, their branches dipping in the water, which is so clear you can see right down to the pebbles lying on the sand. As you go down the steps and walk through the long rustling grass, you can smell the scent of lemon balm and wild violets.

Now you hear sounds, the splash of water against the side of a boat. You look up, shading your eyes from the sunlight. There are people in the boat and one of them is a character you've been having a little trouble with. You want to talk to this character, to hear his or her voice, to ask questions about how s/he feels about the dialogue you've been writing.

Is there something in this character's past you don't know about? Perhaps you have a particular scene that just won't come to life? You could ask the character to help you, maybe act out the scene and tell you what's wrong. Or maybe you just want to have a chat, learn to look at the situation through the character's eyes.

A variation on this visualization is for you to go to the scene of your story and watch the characters in action, in much the same way as a producer might watch actors rehearsing. If a line doesn't sound right, ask the character to change it. The important thing is that the dialogue should be spoken in the characters' own voices. When that dialogue appears on the printed page, it isn't yours; it's theirs. And if those words don't fit, they'll stand out like shell-suits at a royal wedding.

Step Three: from stage to page

Novels are not stage plays. No matter how well we know our characters, how clearly we hear their voices, it will all come to nothing unless we can weave the dialogue with the narrative without leaving holes or ugly seams. Here are some guidelines to help you write the kind of dialogue that looks as if it flowed on to the page like runny honey.

- *Add sensory/scenic detail* Readers need to be able to visualize the characters and their environment, otherwise the dialogue appears to be taking place in a vacuum. That's disorienting for the reader and it also drains realism.

  Our world teems with sensory information: sounds, smells, colours, textures, and tastes, most of which we ignore because we're so used to them. But we'd soon notice if they weren't there – if the sky suddenly turned green or the pavement disappeared. This is why radio plays always have plenty of sound effects, drinks being poured, cars crunching on gravel, the rustle of leaves, and so on.

  In novels, we don't want to bore the readers by describing everything in minute detail. In this passage from *Sons and Lovers*, Paul and Clara talk beside a river. There isn't much description, but it's enough for us to picture the scene:

  > There was the faintest haze over the silvery-dark water and the green meadow banks, and the elm-trees that were spangled with gold. The river slid by in a body, utterly silent and swift, intertwining among itself like some subtle, complex creature...
  >
  > 'Why,' she asked at length, in rather a jarring tone, 'did you leave Miriam?'
  >
  > He frowned.
  >
  > 'Because I *wanted* to leave her,' he said.
  >
  > 'Why?'
  >
  > 'Because I didn't want to go on with her. And I didn't want to marry.'

> She was silent for a moment. They picked their way down the muddy path. Drops of water fell from the elm-trees.
>
> 'You didn't want to marry Miriam, or you didn't want to marry at all?' she asked.

Here, the sensory information comes in two flavours. We have the backdrop: the river, the muddy path, the drops of water from the trees. We also have some detail about the characters: Clara's 'jarring' voice, her silence and Paul's frown.

- **Keep the reader in the picture** Did you notice how Lawrence uses a swift brush-stroke of scenic detail to punctuate the dialogue? In the above passage, it's used as pacing – the characters talk for another half-page. But in any long stretch of dialogue, it's always a good idea to remind the reader from time to time of where they are. If, for example, your characters enter Marble Arch tube station and then talk for the rest of the chapter, readers may forget what's happening and be taken by surprise suddenly to find themselves at Chancery Lane.

- **Blend dialogue with action** In explaining the death of his unfinished first novel, Garrison Keillor says that all the guys in it were 'marathon leaners':

> They leaned against vague vegetation and felt vaguely ill and unhappy, probably the result of their getting no exercise and smoking so many cigarettes. They smoked cigarettes like some people use semi-colons:
>
> 'I'm not sure, not sure at all —' he lit a cigarette and inhaled deeply ⁻— 'perhaps I never will.'

Gratuitous lighting of cigarettes, moving of vases and flicking of imaginary specks of dust are all symptoms of static situations. Sometimes these are unavoidable. If your character's an accountant, for example, you're probably going to have at least one dialogue scene in the office, and there are limits to what one can do in a swivel chair.

It's well worth using your imagination to create scenes in which your characters *are* doing something as well as talking. This will give the dialogue an extra buzz. Maybe your dull accountant could meet a client at one of those posh health clubs where they're both lifting weights or having a massage? In the film *The Thomas Crown Affair*, a chess game is used to mirror the verbal battle between insurance investigator Faye Dunaway and the criminal, Steve McQueen.

In John Grisham's *The Firm*, a Chinese take-away allows Mitch and Abbey McDeere to talk and eat at the same time:

> On the small painted kitchen table, among the legal pads and casebooks, sat a large bottle of wine and a sack of Chinese food. They shoved the law school paraphernalia aside and spread the food. Mitch opened the wine and filled two plastic wineglasses.
>
> 'I had a great interview today,' he said.
>
> 'Who?'
>
> 'Remember that firm in Memphis I received a letter from last month?'
>
> 'Yes. You weren't too impressed.'
>
> 'That's the one. I'm very impressed. It's all tax work and the money looks good.'
>
> 'How good?'
>
> He ceremoniously dipped chow mein from the container onto both plates, then ripped open the tiny packages of soy sauce. She waited for an answer. He opened another container and began dividing the egg foo yung. He sipped his wine and smacked his lips.
>
> 'How much?' she repeated.
>
> 'More than Chicago. More than Wall Street.'

She took a long, deliberate drink of wine and eyed him suspiciously.

Blending dialogue with action will invest your scenes with an illusion of reality, a sense of movement, and, depending on the activity, a touch of originality. You might like to use creative search to give you ideas for keeping your characters' hands busy. To start you off, here are some possibilities:

Icing a cake	Cutting someone's hair
Sailing a boat	Sawing up logs
Painting a mural	Picking fruit off a tree
Mending a motorbike	Oiling a gun
Target shooting	Erecting a tent
Grooming a horse	Feeding an animal, e.g.
Playing snooker	alligator/shark/piranha fish
Sexual foreplay	(think of James Bond)

Try experimenting. Whatever you choose, it's better than an ashtray and a packet of Players.

- **_Vary speech patterns_** If two characters are talking, identify the differences in their style and aim to emphasize those differences. Someone once handed me the manuscript of a novel in which every character used the same swear words – 'Fucking hell', if I remember rightly. It made them sound like children on a school outing.

  In real life we are all products – some might say prisoners – of our own time and experience. Our speech reflects this in a myriad different ways. If a teenager is talking to his grandfather, for example, the readers should be able to guess who's talking from their personal style: the words they choose and the way they arrange them. The grandfather may use longer, more pontifical sentences, while the teenager may use slang and the current idiom.

Don't misunderstand me. I'm not saying that all grand-fathers are the same. A grandfather who was himself a teenager in the late 1950s/early 1960s will speak very differently from one who was born pre-war.

The following stripped-down dialogue from Deborah Moggach's *Close to Home* occurs between a teenage girl and a man in his thirties, whom the girl madly fancies. No prizes for guessing who says what:

> 'Lovely day. Will the weather ever break?'
> 'It's lovely and hot. I like it hot like this.'
> 'One certainly shouldn't complain. It really is quite remarkable for England, isn't it?'
> 'Oh, yes. Yes.'
> 'Soon, no doubt, someone will be complaining about the sun.'
> 'Wouldn't that be funny!'

Here, the girl's youthful gaucheness is reflected in her clumsy repetitions and her stilted 'Oh, yes. Yes.' The man is at ease with small talk; she is not. Passion has clouded her ability to communicate. One can practically see her blushing and fidgeting. Now take a look at what Deborah Moggach actually wrote:

> 'Lovely day,' he said. 'Will the weather ever break?'
> 'It's lovely and hot,' she said stupidly.
> A silence. Just the clack of their footsteps. She looked down at her legs, fat and pale. She racked her brains for something to say.
> 'I like it hot like this,' she said. Half an hour ago she had been in his arms [in her imagination]. They had been in a little summerhouse, to be exact, on a wooden bench. Marion blushed.
> He said: 'One certainly shouldn't complain. It really is quite remarkable for England, isn't it?'

'Oh, yes,' she said. 'Yes.'

Their footsteps clacked on, side by side. She almost wished this meeting could be got over quickly so she could think about it.

'Soon, no doubt,' he said, 'someone will be complaining about the sun.'

'Wouldn't that be funny!' Marion's squeaky laugh startled her …

Another thing to remember is that our speech patterns vary according to whom we're talking to. There's an interesting story about Lloyd George, who apparently would absorb the personality of anyone he was with and 'become' them. This raised the question of what he was like when alone. The answer (from one of his enemies): 'When Lloyd George is in a room alone, the room is empty.'

Most of us probably aren't quite that bad, but you only have to listen to an adult trying to converse with a baby, or small child, to see this principle in action. Men who are absolute tyrants at work may be sweet as honey to their wives. Adolescents who can't string two civil words together for their parents will be different people to their friends.

- *Let dialogue be choppy* Ford Maddox Ford said that no speech of one character should ever answer the speech that goes before it. That's an exaggeration, but the point is a good one. What he's saying is that most of us hear only the beginning of what others say to us because we're too busy framing our reply.

It's true. When people volunteer to run crisis hot-lines or become counsellors, they have to be taught how to listen. It's not easy. And the effect is accentuated in emotive situations, when we're angry, for example, upset, or even blissfully happy. Consequently, smooth dialogue in which each character takes their turn and always waits for the other to finish sounds stilted and unrealistic.

Dialogue that sounds natural will contain interruptions, jumps of thought, and the odd unanswered question. In this passage from Jonathan Kellerman's *Silent Partner*, the main character is a child psychologist talking to a mother about her maladjusted son:

'There's plenty of fear and anger still in him. It would help him to express it. I'd like to see him some more.'

She looked at the ceiling.

'Those dolls,' she said.

'I know. It's hard to watch.'

She bit her lip.

'But it's helpful for Darren, Denise. We can try having you wait outside next time. He's ready for it.'

She said, 'It's far, coming up here.'

'Bad traffic?'

'The pits.'

'How long did it take you?'

'Hour and three quarters.'

Tujunga to Beverley Glen. A forty-minute freeway ride. If you could handle freeways.

'Surface streets jammed?'

'Uh huh. And you've got some curvy roads up here.'

'I know. Sometimes when–'

Suddenly she was backing away. 'Why do you make your-self so hard to get to, living up here! If you want to help people, why do you make it so damned hard!'

I waited a moment before answering. 'I know it's been rough, Denise. If you'd rather meet me in Mr Worthy's—'

'Oh, forget it!' And she was out the door.

The attitude of the professional carer is mirrored in his speech. He's patient. He listens. By contrast, Denise is adrift in her own anxious thoughts. She doesn't hear. She interrupts. She asks questions to which she doesn't really want an answer. Note how the author has replaced question marks with exclamation marks: 'If you want to help people, why do you make it so damned hard!' This is the sort of dialogue which makes a best-seller.

Some common mistakes

Don't be too explicit

We had an example of this in the excruciating dialogue at the beginning of the chapter. (You might like to page back and read it to refresh your memory.) If you find yourself using dialogue to explain to the reader things that the characters would already know, stop. For example, if a woman comes home in the evening and her husband says, 'Hello, Sandy, how was your day at the hospital?' you might ask yourself why he needs to remind her of where she works.

And if Sandy goes on to say, 'Well, as you know, we've been moving the surgical patients into the new wing,' you might question why she needs to tell him again. The reader will pick up on this because it sounds contrived. It's like those 1950s TV commercials in which a lady in a nice dress says: 'Now, Malcolm, how can we stop paint dripping on our hands when we're emulsioning the ceiling?'

If it's important for the reader to know immediately that Sandy's a nurse, find some other way of showing it. She could smell of antiseptic. She could relate a funny story about one of the doctors. She could go upstairs to change out of her uniform. Remember, too, that readers don't have to know everything right *now*.

Don't get dotty

'Oh, Debbie, do you think we could…?'
  'Darling, I thought you'd never ask, but…'
  'I know what you're thinking. It's such a big step and…'

'No, it's not that, it's just ...'
'It's the time, isn't it, it's not ...'

You get the picture? Too many dots make the text look like measles. Don't confuse realism with a mess on the page.

No long speeches

This is the opposite of going 'dotty'. If your character has a lot to say, you may feel tempted to let him or her deliver it in a single lump. Resist. Firstly, if a character hogs centre-stage without pause or interruption, the dialogue will lose its impact and start to sound like narration. This will slow your story.

Secondly, psychologists have discovered that when people are concentrating they absorb information in the following order: last, first and middle. Consequently, what your character says in the middle of the dialogue may well be forgotten. If you want it forgotten, fine. In fact, this is a useful technique for 'hiding' information that you want to use later (we'll talk more about this in the plotting section).

Thirdly, big chunks of dialogue will make your pages look heavy.

Don't take your readers through passport-control

'Hi, I haven't seen you before.'
'No, my family's just moved here from the south. My father's taken over the foundry.'
'What's your name?'
'Isobel.'
'Glad to meet you. I'm Greta, from number 44.'

When characters first meet, it's easy to get bogged down in this kind of question-and-answer session. It's a touch clumsy. Although it tells us about the characters, it's not particularly interesting. In fact, readers don't give a toss about characters until the writer's done something to stimulate their curiosity. Try asking yourself:

1 Do my readers need this information?
2 Do they need it right now?

In most cases, the answer to the second question will be No. The solution is to wait until these two characters are involved in a significant scene in which you can then blend the information with action.

Don't show off

I only mention this because someone once handed me a manuscript in which the dialogue was peppered with literary allusions. For some reason, the writer seemed to think that this would impress the reader. Trust me, the kind of reader who's going to be impressed won't understand what you're on about; and the kind who does understand will think you're a poser. If your character is a poser, it's fine to have him break into fancy French phrases at the drop of a croissant. Dialogue that's there to boost the writer's ego is like a blunt pencil – pointless.

Don't repeat

In real life, we repeat ourselves all the time. It's our way of familiarizing ourselves with our subject. In fiction, there are only two valid reasons for dialogue that repeats itself:

1 As a character tag
2 To emphasize the significance of something important.

9

Finding a Plot

If you're reading this, white-faced and trembling, with a triple gin in one hand and a cigarette in the other – relax. I know that many of you find dreaming up plots an elusive skill to master, but there's a lot we can do to get the process bubbling. Let's start with a pep talk.

Don't waste your time looking for a plot that's never been used. There are none out there. Fiction is like the fashion business. It's been around so long that almost everything is derivative. Take Vivienne Westwood, a designer most of us would regard as a bit different (or completely loco, depending on your point of view). Look at her clothes. Those collars shaped like toy dogs' tongues were around in the 1960s, her bum cushion is a Victorian bustle, and the fig-leaf in her body stocking was a big hit in the Garden of Eden.

Does that damage her reputation as one of the world's wackiest designers? No. As Lajos Egri says: 'In the arts ... we cannot discover startling originality – only trends, styles, twists, slants, tricks, exaggeration, minimization, emphasis on parts instead of a whole.'

This emphasis on *parts* instead of the *whole* is the basis of all creativity, plotting included. Just as Westwood might take a plain dress and cover it with chicken wire, so can writers take a basic plot and develop it afresh.

For example, you might not expect to find much correlation between classical literature and a category romance. Yet, when social psychologist Janice Radway studied the narrative structure of popular romances, she found it was the same as in *Jane Eyre* and *Pride and Prejudice*. Step Seven, for example, is: 'Hero and heroine are physically and/or emotionally separated – leads to hero fearing he may lose her.'

The actual circumstances of this parting are different in every book, but they are there just the same. (You'll find the other steps listed in Radway's book, *Reading the Romance: Women, Patriarchy and Popular Literature*.)

For any modern novel, it's never the plot itself that makes the content original. It's the treatment the author gives it.

Of course, you can start from scratch, and later on we'll be discussing ways to generate ideas. But if you're the kind of writer for whom a blank page is as scary as the shower scene in *Psycho*, it will help you to build up a library of basic plots that you can pull out when you're desperate. Some people call these dramatic situations or plot patterns. A book worth looking at is *20 Master Plots*, by Ronald B. Tobias. Each plot pattern carries a brief label: 'Quest', for example, or 'Rivalry'. The author goes on to discuss each plot, with specific examples. It's an interesting read, but no substitute for your own research.

Building up a plot library

Even if you haven't yet got around to thinking about plot, you probably have a fair idea of what sort of novel you want to write. If not, it might be helpful to think about this. At present, publishers are more likely to accept a novel if it fits into one of their recognized genres: thriller, mystery, horror, romance, sci-fi.

Within these genres, there are sub-divisions. At the time

of writing, erotica – or as one critic put it, loveless sex – for women is selling well, as are psychological thrillers, full of violence and suspense. By the time you read this, who knows? Things are always changing. Even if your aim is simply to write a damn good novel, it pays to look around the shelves to see what's on offer.

The first step is to select some books in your chosen sphere. I suggest they be modern ones. There are fashions in plots and you want to know what's selling *now*. This doesn't mean that we can't learn from the classics, but bear in mind that all authors are products of their own time. If Dickens, for example, were alive today, his books would reflect a very different world.

You don't have to read these books all the way through. Very often, the blurb on the back will tell you enough to identify the plot.

Max Byrd is a thriller writer who used this technique to identify seven major plot categories. For example, the 'ticking clock' plot, exemplified by Michael Crichton's *The Andromeda Strain*, uses the device of a deadline to build up suspense. Will the experts manage to stop the deadly bacterium before it destroys mankind? Will the secret weapon be found before it's too late? The variations are endless.

Another category is the 'caper', in which the plot consists mainly of the protagonist's preparations to achieve his goal. A famous example is *The Day of the Jackal*: an unnamed Englishman makes plans to assassinate the president of France.

As you categorize books in this way, you may be surprised to find how few basic plots there are. It's the same with romance. A perennial favourite is the 'Romeo and Juliet' plot in which lovers are kept apart by a family feud. That wasn't new when Shakespeare used it but it's still fuelling new stories.

Keep track of all these plots, either in a notebook or on index cards. Whenever you pick up a book, identify its category and add it to your list, with a few brief details to show what the writer has done to clothe the bare bones.

Every now and again you may come across a new category or possibly two categories blended into one. There are no rules in this game.

Remember that the author will have used particularizing details to disguise the basic plot, in much the same way as we might disguise ourselves by wearing a mask and a wig. Think of the gripping finale to all those James Bond films. Bond tracks the villain to his headquarters – the jungle lair, the high-tech space module, the undersea headquarters that looked like a Blue Peter project for using up egg-boxes. They're all the same; they just *look* different.

Identifying themes

When plots are reduced to their skeletons, we call them themes, particularly the ones that can be expressed in a single word, such as revenge or betrayal. A novel will always have a main theme, a thread that holds the story together, which answers the question: What, in a nutshell, is this story about? For example, the main theme of Maeve Haran's blockbuster *Having It All* is the conflicts faced by women who want a career and a family.

Most novels, however, also have internal, or subsidiary themes, and to find these we have to read the whole book. These themes are like repeating elements in a pattern which contribute to the mood and character throughout the story. For example, in Joanna Trollope's *The Spanish Lover*, there are themes of possessiveness and guilt, motherhood, marriage and late flowering with a vengeance.

Many well-known writers are inspired by themes, including Minette Walters whose first book, *The Ice House*, won the John Creasey Award for Best First Crime Novel of the Year. She's fascinated, she says, by the damage that families can do to themselves, and the nature of truth.

Similarly, crime writer Harry Keating finds that what fires his imagination is the underlying theme. He relates the experience of going into his local grocery shop and seeing a lady wearing (it was obvious to him) a rubber corset. He suddenly saw this as a willingness, or desire, to be restricted. He then asked himself how this could possibly come into the world of his detective, Inspector Ghote: 'And then I thought: Oh, yes, Indian dancers; the very opposite of the lady in the rubber corset.'

One word of caution. Use theme to generate ideas, not to control them. Sometimes, writers will tell me they want to explore the theme of urban pollution, say, or growing up in an alien environment. This is fine, but the theme must always be subservient to the individual experiences of your characters. When authors get carried away by a theme, particularly if it's a cause or issue about which they feel strongly, the characters are demoted to puppets whose only purpose is to promote the author's viewpoint. The book then stops being a story and becomes propaganda.

Take a tip from John Mortimer: 'The novelist has a duty which he must perform before he starts illuminating the human condition. He must entertain the audience.'

An exercise in themes

Pick a book, preferably one you've enjoyed, and make a list of all the themes, both main and internal. You'll find this particularly rewarding when analysing stories that delve into human nature and the relationships between people. In literary novels, for example, you won't find fast action in the form of car chases or races against time. Rather the plot will focus on the minds of the characters.

Let's have a look at some of the ways in which the exercise will help you:

- In probing beyond the surface structure of a book, you'll get a feel for its structure, and how the author has clothed it. You'll be able to relate the themes to the plot, see how they've been woven together. For example, if there's a theme of family loyalty, where are the scenes that illustrate this? What effect do they have on the subsequent action?

- Having analysed a published book, you'll be better able to apply the same analysis to your own novel. You may then detect flaws that would otherwise go unnoticed.

- It's always illuminating to see the range of themes used by other authors and the different treatments they give them. I once had a student who wanted to write a Robert Hale romance. I researched twenty titles and discovered that approximately 50 per cent contained the same initial theme: a heroine with an insecure past. Another common theme was the independence of woman against powerful man. I've no doubt that I'd have discovered more on actually reading the books.

  Don't think I'm suggesting this as an argument for constructing a book to a formula. Writers should be free to write the book they want. However, if a theme crops up regularly, it probably means the readers like it. And as they say, he who pays the piper ...

- If, as I suggested, you chose a book you've enjoyed, the themes running through it are probably the same themes you should think of exploring in your own novel. This doesn't mean that your book will be a clone of one written by your favourite author. Every theme has an infinite number of variations. For example, Golding's *Lord of the*

Flies and L. P. Hartley's *The Go-Between* are both examples of the coming-of-age/rites-of-passage theme. The plots, however, are totally unalike.

The same theme has been used countless times by Hollywood for such films as *Rebel Without a Cause*, *Stand by Me*, and *St Elmo's Fire*.

It's not hard to see why this theme is so popular. Adolescence is something we all go through. It's an emotional time: conflict with our parents, our friends, and our own hormones which suddenly boil up like a pan of rice pudding. So, although the plots illustrating the theme may be different from our own personal experience, we can all identify with the problems involved.

Once you have identified a few themes which interest you, you may like to do a creative search to give you ideas. Just stick the theme in the middle of your page and go from there. You never know; you might come up with the bones of your very first published novel.

Plotting from your own experience

Trust me, you are your own richest source of plotting ideas. Yes, even if you've lived in the same town all your life, have never been abroad, and work in a factory that produces the spacers for ceramic wall tiles.

Oh sure, there are some writers who were once secret agents, or photographic models, but they're the exceptions. The point about most successful novelists is that they don't live in the real world at all. I mean what's *real* about sitting at a desk for hours on end, with only imaginary people for company? As John Fowles once observed, 'There are many reasons why novelists write – but they all have one thing in common: a need to create an alternative world.'

But wait a minute. Blockbuster novels are full of glamorous jet-setters, exotic locations and wall-to-wall testosterone. Am I trying to pretend that a group of randy office clerks in Croydon will work the same magic?

Not exactly. What I am saying is probably best contained in a line by Sir Philip Sidney: ' "Fool," said my Muse to me; "look in thy heart and write." '

Fiction is about *people* and the problems they face. If you can engage your readers' emotions, involve them with your characters, your novel will be a success whether it's set in San Francisco or Southend. It won't be a 'Jackie Collins' or a 'Wilbur Smith', but it will still be a book that gives people pleasure.

Remember, too, that there's a difference between experience and research. Many of our most popular authors are able to write the books they do because they now have the time and money to immerse themselves in their subject. Hunter S. Thomson ran with the Hell's Angels for eighteen months just so he could write about them. Jackie Collins went on the road with a heavy-metal group for her novel, *Rockstar*. For *Devil's Juggler*, Murray Smith spent over £100,000 researching the drug baronies of Colombia. Included in his expenses was the hire of a bodyguard!

But not all blockbuster novels are set in a rarefied world. Barbara Taylor Bradford was in the middle of writing a suspense novel set in New York and Spain when she ran out of steam: 'I got to Chapter Four and I thought, this is boring. I asked myself a lot of questions that day. I said: well, what do you want to write about? What sort of book do you want to write? Where do you want to set it?'

The result of this heart-searching was *A Woman of Substance*, set in her home county of Yorkshire. And the rest, as they say is history.

You may be cheered by what best-selling novelist Rosie Thomas has to say: 'The glitzy, shopping-and-fucking, bitch-in-the-boardroom that was so popular in the 1980s is *out* now. People want relationships and reality.' Her own latest novel,

Other People's Marriages, is about small-town marital infidelity.

If you really want to write a novel that's outside your own sphere of experience, wait until you can afford to do the research. In the meantime, get yourself some street cred. Write a good novel *now*, using your own life experience as source material.

Don't think I'm suggesting you write your autobiography. It's true that many first novels are thinly disguised autobiographies, but novels that set out to be such are usually failures, mainly because the author has forgotten that fiction is supposed to be entertainment.

Remember the poor miller's daughter in the folk-tale *Rumpelstiltskin*? She took straw and spun it into gold. We too can take the straw of our lives, and let our imaginations turn it into the gold of our plots. Let's look at how some popular authors use their own experience to fuel their stories:

- The straw for Helen Zahavi's first novel, *Dirty Weekend*, came from her own fear. At the time, she was living alone in a flat in a rough area of Brighton. Many local women had been raped; Helen herself was receiving obscene phone calls. She went out and bought herself a gun. But she was still terrified.

  Then, early one morning – about 2 o'clock – she got out of bed and stood at her window, staring at the block of flats across from hers. In one of them was her would-be attacker (he'd told her he was watching her). For the first time, she confronted her fear. She asked herself what would happen if she stopped being a victim and became instead a perpetrator. What if she killed the man who was threatening her? In her imagination this felt good, and at that moment her book was born. Its first line reads: 'This is the story of Bella, who woke up one morning and realised she'd had enough.'

Helen Zahavi's is the kind of success story about which all

writers dream. While the book was still in galley proof, Michael Winner saw it and decided to film it. It has since been short-listed for the Whitbread Prize and translated into eleven languages.

And it all started with the author's fear.

Why not try a creative search on your own fears? What brings you out in a cold sweat? Rats? Dead bodies? Closed-in spaces? Or perhaps the thought of growing old? Whatever fear you choose, the chances are that your readers will relate to it. And reading about it will help to release their own latent fears.

Once you have a fear, play around with it to get ideas. In Helen Zahavi's case, she used the what-if? technique. You can do the same. Suppose your fear is fire. What if you're at the top of a tall building when it catches fire? This idea became a film, *The Towering Inferno*.

What if those crows on the telegraph wire suddenly became vicious? Daphne du Maurier used this in *The Birds*, which also became a film. Similarly, *Arachnophobia* explored the nightmarish scenario of a plague of killer spiders.

- Caring about something deeply is a good reason to write about it. Maeve Haran had already written an unsuccessful sex-and-shopping novel when her agent suggested she write about something she personally cared about. At the time, she was trying to juggle her career as a television producer with that of bringing up her children: 'I sat around thinking for a long time and then I realised, well, there's one thing everybody I know talks about all the time, which is how you balance work and children.... After that the novel sort of wrote itself.'

  Margaret Forster's novel *Have the Men had Enough?* arose out of anger at her mother-in-law's treatment in the geriatric ward of a mental hospital: 'I despised myself for not *doing* anything, for not storming, yelling at whoever ran those hideous wards.... So I thought I would write a novel after she died, that I would try to use the novel as a vehicle to express my rage and explore the whole dilemma.' The book took her six weeks to write.

Dick Francis's wife, Mary, contracted polio and was confined for a time to an artificial respirator. She recovered, but the experience left a big impression on Francis. He used it in *Forfeit*, a novel in which the main character's wife is also paralysed but does not recover.

Is there some area of your life that you'd like to explore, some injustice, some problem that you might share with others? Even if you don't use this as your main theme, it will get you started and may help to spark ideas. Again, try a creative search on 'Things I care about' and see what comes up.

- Many writers find inspiration in their careers. Jonathan Kellerman is a child psychologist. Scott Turow (of *Presumed Innocent* fame) is a lawyer, as is John Grisham. Claire Rayner was a nurse. Miss Read was a teacher. All use their professions as grist for their writing. If you don't have a profession, what about odd jobs? Crime writer Liza Cody once worked at Madame Tussaud's, putting the hairs on the waxworks' heads. Both this and a short time as a rock group's roadie crop up in her writing.

   Don't overlook the careers of your friends either. Cultivate acquaintances who might be able to help you. One of my students had a lucky break when the police arrested him for a crime he hadn't committed. Later, when he told them he was a writer, they told him to drop by if he wanted to know anything. This was fortunate as he does write crime novels.

- For Ruth Rendell, an interest in Jungian psychology has fuelled the suspense novels written under her Barbara

Vine pseudonym. In her own life, she admits that she often feels that personal disaster is imminent, some kind of disgrace, humiliation, suffering, pain, poverty, famine. 'It is a neurotic state. I wish I didn't have it. I have it.'

As Julian Symonds points out in his book *Bloody Murder*, many of Rendell's characters have it too and it appears in her books as a flaw in the personality that leads to violence when put under some kind of emotional stress. The basis of this flaw is often sexual. *Demon in My View*, for example, is about a man who keeps a dummy woman in his cellar and takes pleasure in strangling her every few days.

Kurt Vonnegut said that writers can treat their mental illnesses every day. He's right, and we shouldn't knock writing as an outlet for our hang-ups. Anthony Storr, a psychiatrist who has studied the links between creativity and 'madness', claims that 'Creativity is one mode adopted by gifted people of coming to terms with, or finding solutions for, the internal tensions and dissociations from which all human beings suffer in varying degree.'

If you have some particular neuroses, why not use them in your writing? You'll be in good company.

• In many novels, environment provides the necessary catalyst. Garrison Keillor's novel *Lake Wobegon Days* is a comic study of a fictitious little town in the writer's home state of Minnesota. In Margaret Mitchell's classic *Gone with the Wind*, the American Civil War as it affected the state of Georgia is central to the plot.

Hampshire writer Betty Burton's new historical saga was inspired by her interest in Portsmouth's corset-making industry: 'I placed an advertisement in the local paper in order to contact women who had worked in the corset factories. I was flooded with replies.... They were so absorbing that this is a book I just have to write.'

Why not take a fresh look at your home town? If it has a museum, go visit it. Is there a particular street or area that might provide a background for your story? What sort of plot can you imagine hatching there? It's probably no coincidence that Jilly Cooper's Gloucestershire horsey novels came out after she moved to the country from Putney. Similarly, Colin Dexter explores the Jericho area of Oxford for his tales about Inspector Morse.

• According to Freud, dreaming liberates the imagination, and many great writers list dreams as the source of their ideas. Mary Shelley's *Frankenstein* was based on a nightmare. Robert Louis Stevenson already had the theme for his *The Strange Case of Doctor Jekyll and Mr Hyde*, but was stuck for a plot. Then, one night: 'I dreamed the scene at the window, and a scene afterwards split in two, in which Hyde, pursued for some crime, took the powder, and underwent the change in the presence of his pursuers.'

Dreams work because they come from our subconscious, the compost heap of our lives. If you want to cultivate creative dreaming, the trick is to think a lot about your story while you're awake and then, at night, to give yourself a positive suggestion that you're going to have a useful dream. In the morning, immediately on waking, record your dream.

Don't be disheartened if it doesn't work first time. One of my students who tried this method reported no immediate success. Instead of giving up, she persevered, each night telling herself firmly, 'Tonight I'm going to dream, and in the morning I'll remember.'

Eventually, it worked. The dream, which was in colour, was of a room in Paris. My student saw tall windows, oak floorboards, maroon velvet curtains, a massive mirror framed in gold leaf, and a brocade *chaise longue* on which she, herself, was lying. In the dream, she woke to see a wizened old woman who told her she'd had a miscarriage. At the time, my student was writing a series of stories involving pregnancy and that vivid dream become an opening scene.

For more information on dreams and how to control them, try reading *Lucid Dreams in 30 Days*, by Keith Harary and Pamela Weintraub.

More plotting ideas

Newspapers

Newspapers are wonderful sources of plot ideas. Penny Vincenzi was a journalist who wanted to write a novel, but thought she'd never quite crack it. Then: 'I stumbled on this idea from an item about wills in the *Mail on Sunday*. Somebody had done something very peculiar and left everything to a very distant relative – it made me think that wills are amazing things for manipulation. So I just began.'

Many writers fill shoeboxes with interesting clippings and simply leaf through them when they want an idea. Remember, though, the clipping is just the seed of your plot; it's up to you to add foliage and form. It took Penny Vincenzi two years to get her book to the point at which a publisher was interested enough to offer an advance.

An interesting exercise is to select two news items and blend them together. Peter Lovesey's historical crime novel *The Last Detective* was inspired by the juxtaposition of a murder report and that of a swimming accident.

Why not try a clippings lucky dip? Select two or even three items at random and try to connect them.

Overheard conversations

Most writers eavesdrop on the conversations of others. Snippets work best. Hilary Mantel was once standing at a bus stop when she overheard two women talking about the goings-on at a local youth club. One of them said: 'They stole my skeleton, you know.' The other replied: 'Yes, good job it wasn't a full-sized one.' Later, Mantel wrote *Vacant Possession* in which a group of children wander around the north of England with a set of under-sized bones.

Become an oyster

The oyster finds a grain of sand and builds a pearl around the grain. You can do the same. Write a scene, or a snatch of dialogue. Stick it on a spike and add more scenes or ideas as they occur to you. Ruth Elwyn Harris started with a basic idea of four sisters, three of whom painted while the fourth did not. She visualized scenes and conversations and wrote these down just as they came. When she'd accumulated enough, she put them into an order that seemed to make sense. The resulting novel was *The Silent Shore*, the first of a trilogy.

Vladimir Nabokov is another writer who wrote without order or chronology. He used index cards to record his plot ideas, shuffling them around until he found an arrangement that pleased him. Then he gave the cards to his wife who went off and typed them. His novel *Lolita* was a great success.

Try the romantic approach

Just start writing. John Mortimer was encouraged to try this when he heard about Georges Feydeau, a French writer of farces whose 'plots are as intricate and precisely fashioned as the inside of a gold watch. Surely his plays had to be meticulously planned?' No. Apparently, Feydeau started to write with no idea of what was going to happen. 'But soon he began to create such tempting characters and situations that plots came rushing to his aid.'

As Mortimer points out, plots are notoriously shy and retiring, but the clatter of a typewriter can often spring them into action.

First find the end

John Irving claims he always begins his novels at the end and works backwards. It's a control thing, he says. He must know what happens before he can proceed. Margaret Mitchell actually wrote *Gone with the Wind* backwards, starting with the last chapter. It's an interesting approach and just might work for you. Try thinking of your climax scene and what might have led up to it.

Start with an intriguing situation

This could be anything. John Wyndam's *The Day of the Triffids* opens with the main character waking up after an eye operation to find that only he can see. Everyone else has gone blind. In Scott Smith's *A Simple Plan*, three men stumble across the wreckage of an aircraft and a duffel bag containing $4.4 million. Here are some more ideas:

- Two teenagers steal a car and later find a dead woman in the boot.

- A man comes home to find his wife missing. There is no note and no clothes are missing from her wardrobe.

- A woman is waiting for a visit from her sister – who never arrives. According to the police, her sister was mown down by a car after having consumed a lot of alcohol. But the woman knows her sister doesn't drink.

Do a creative search
on a single word

Have you noticed how many novels have single word titles? *Destiny, Money, Kidnapped, Damage, Rivals.* Notice how these words provoke questions before the reader has even opened the book. Whose destiny? Who are the rivals? What's damaged? If single words can stimulate the reader's curiosity, we as writers can use them to generate ideas.

Shirley Conran's first novel sprang into life from a single word. At the time, she was on a promotional tour for *Superwoman.* Alone on her birthday, cocooned in the luxury of an American hotel, she felt depressed: 'I thought I must do something positive – that's the way to counter depression.' So she wrote the word 'Lace'. This prompted a few characters and the sentence: 'Which of you bitches is my mother?' Then she scribbled a synopsis on her telephone message pad.

When choosing a word, go for one that's likely to stimulate an emotive response. Here are some suggestions:

Power	Lust	Desire
Guilt	Promise	Possession
Ransom	Secret	Revenge
Waiting	Fate	Forbidden

Before tackling your own search, read the following examples which two creative writing students completed in a ten-minute exercise. Both started from the word LUST, but, as you can see, the results are very different.

He looked around for a chair on which to sit, but the bedroom was too small to contain anything more than the bed, a dresser and a single wardrobe, so he perched himself self-consciously on the edge of the bed, and watched her as she washed her hair. She had long, raven-black hair, cut to a fringe at the front, but reaching down behind to the small

Student Example No. 1

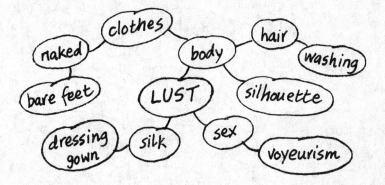

of her back. Clearly, washing her hair was hard work. She stood, bending over the small basin, her silk dressing gown stretched taut across her back and buttocks. A thought suddenly struck him. She had told him once, casually, that she always washed her hair stark naked because it was so long and unmanageable. Now, looking more closely, he could see the silhouette of her body through the thin material. He stood up and pretended to examine the clutter of objects on the dresser. From the side, her gown hung open, pushed apart by her breasts to reveal one deep-rose nipple, her legs slightly apart as she crouched over the basin. She was bare footed, and he was struck by how small she was – he had never seen her without her shoes on before – and he realised that she must always wear high heels to counteract her lack of height.

He saw her body stiffen. She had sensed his gaze. Moving casually back towards the bed, he had a sudden desire to step behind her, to slip his hands inside her dressing gown, caressing and cupping her breasts, imagining what would come next. But then he stopped, overcome by the fear of rejection, realising the enormity of the risk he was taking.   *Simon Heath*

Student Example No. 2

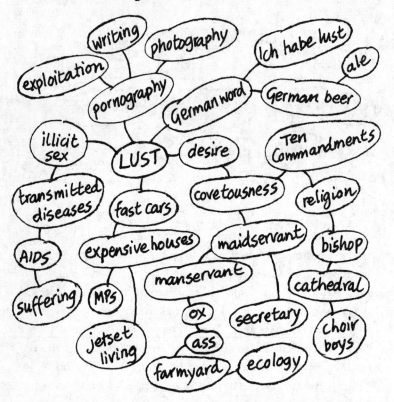

(Note: This writer spent more time on his creative search, thereby stimulating ideas that could not be developed in a single scene. With only three minutes left, he nevertheless managed to pull some of those ideas together as the bones of a plot. Tongue-in-cheek it may be, but imagine it in the hands of a comic writer such as Tom Sharpe and you'll see the possibilities.)

A bishop and a local MP have become acquainted. The bishop has a seat in the House of Lords and the MP wants his support for a motion initiated in the Lords.

The MP (sixty, with a failing marriage) fancies the bishop's eighteen-year-old daughter, while the bishop fancies the MP's twenty-five-year-old secretary.

The archdeacon fancies a young curate who has just been appointed to an admin position in the cathedral offices, but the curate fancies several of the boys in the cathedral choir. The bishop's wife fancies the young curate. The ancient cathedral verger fancies a pint of real ale.

James Carter

10

Assembling Your Plot

Once you have an idea for your plot, it's time to develop it. Few plots come into being fully-formed so don't worry if yours seems a touch nebulous. John Irving's novel *A Son of the Circus* started with a single image: a well-dressed man, 'Indian or Middle Eastern or Persian', standing on the corner of a street in Toronto. The author saw him from a taxi cab, stopped at a red light: 'I began just imagining that sense of the foreignness of the life he had come from, which is invisible to most of the people who would know him in his adopted country, but also how foreign we must seem to him.'

Then the light changed to green ... and Irving started to dream.

Writers often ask me about outlines. Is it essential to do a chapter-by-chapter breakdown? By all means, if the idea appeals to you. Some writers, such as Ken Follett, Frederick Forsyth and Celia Brayfield, make detailed synopses. These may run up to thirty pages long and are revised and refined until the author is satisfied.

Other writers just write. 'The first draft,' says Booker Prize-winner Michael Ondaatje, 'is more of a searching, a kind of discovery. I don't have a great plan beforehand. I don't work things out at the beginning, but I spend twice as much time at the end, making sure I have a structure that is tight.'

Even Murray Smith (he of the £100,000 research expenses) says that he came home and wrote the first fifty pages of *The Devil's Juggler* without being sure where his plot was going. He didn't even know the identity of the corpse that appears at the start of the story: 'In fact, I didn't really know, until the last five pages, just how the whole thing was going to end.'

So, there you are. It's up to you. What is important is to think about your plot. Do as John Irving did – carry on dreaming. Play around with ideas. Let your mind roam over possibilities. Ask questions. Incubation is an important part of the creative process. Provide your unconscious with enough material and it will set to work on reorganizing it, making connections that you hadn't thought of.

Raymond Chandler once said, 'A good story cannot be devised; it has to be distilled.' In the end, it doesn't really matter whether that distillation process takes place on paper, in your brain, or a combination of the two.

This is the creative part of writing, and while it's going on your right brain should be free to wander without any distracting criticism. Eventually, though, you'll need to think about mechanics, the structural components that will turn your ideas into something the readers can recognize when they pick up your novel.

What you'll find in this chapter are the basic ingredients. In Chapter Eleven, we'll discuss some special techniques.

Basic ingredients

The hook

A common fault is to start a story too soon – perhaps with the lead character getting out of bed and taking a shower. This is understandable. After all, we want to set the scene, to let the reader know what's what.

No, we don't. Stand in any bookshop and watch what happens when someone picks up a novel. First they look at the cover, then they glance at the back to see what Stephen King (or some other trusted author) thought of the story. Finally, they open the book and read the first paragraph.

At that moment, the author has approximately five seconds to persuade the potential reader to buy the book. If the reader doesn't like what s/he sees, that's the end of the line. You never get a second chance to make a good first impression.

This, then, is the purpose, of your beginning: to draw the reader into the world of your imaginings. There's no point in being subtle. The reader wants to be seduced or s/he would-n't be here.

Many writers have difficulty identifying the best place to start. It's not hard to see why. Real life is a continuum which begins when we're born and doesn't stop until we die. Fiction, however, is finite, and few modern stories begin with the hero's or heroine's first lusty cries.

It may help to think of your story as having two possible beginnings. One is the chronological or 'natural' beginning, the point at which you might say, 'It all started when....' The second is the actual beginning of the story on the page. Let me explain.

The natural beginning is – and I'd like to emphasize this – a moment of change, a crisis point in the lives of the characters. For example, imagine that a married couple have been rubbing along together in semi-discontent for a number of years. That's the norm of their lives, so no story there. Then, something happens to trigger a change. In Kingsley Amis's *The Old Devils*, for example, a woman from the past arrives to disrupt the present. In Alice Thomas Ellis's *The Other Side of the Fire*, the main character suddenly realizes she's fallen in love with her step-son.

The nature of the trigger could be anything. What's important is that it creates conflict for the main character, who must now make a decision or take some action.

Learn to look for the trigger point in your story ideas. Then, unless there's good reason not to, start your story right there. Fill in background details later, when the readers are involved.

For some stories, however, the trigger point is not the best place to start. The trigger point in Daphne du Maurier's *Rebecca*, for example, would be the heroine's first meeting with Maxim de Winter, the man she marries and accompanies to Manderley. In the author's original synopsis, this *is* where it begins. The actual book, however, begins long after the action is over, with the heroine dreaming of those past events, reflecting on the horror.

Why would we, as writers, choose to follow this example? The simple answer is: to tantalize the readers, to whet their appetites, to wind up the tension. It's a popular technique with thriller writers who want the readers to know that nasty things are in store.

The trigger point and the end are not the only options. Technically, you can start wherever you want. As a guide, try looking at the story from the reader's point of view. Ask yourself: will my reader be able to follow this? Is this confusing? If the answer's Yes, think again.

Having decided on where to start your story, you are now faced with another decision. What type of opening are you going to choose?

A tried and tested option is to start with action. Romantic suspense writer Phyllis A. Whitney suggests you make it as personal as possible. 'Impersonal action, however busy and violent, doesn't necessarily hold a reader. You need to have some personal human connection before the reader will care.'

Let's see if she's right.

I was in deep sleep, alone aboard my houseboat, alone in the half acre of bed, alone in a sweaty dream of chase, fear and monstrous predators. A shot rang off steel bars. Another. I came bursting up out of sleep to hear the secretive sound of the little bell which rings at my bedside when anyone steps aboard *The Busted Flush*. It was almost four in the morning.

It could be some kid prowling the decks for a forgotten camera, portable radio, or bottle of Scotch. Or a friendly drunk. Or a drunken friend. Or trouble.

Here, John D. McDonald plunges us straight into *The Dreadful Lemon Sky*. Something is happening and we want to know what. The author doesn't bother with explanation. However, he gives us more information than first appears. For a start, those short sentences build tension. So we know there's trouble on the way.

We know, too, that the protagonist is no Sunday sailor. Ordinary people don't dream of shots ringing off steel bars. Similarly, the boat is called *The Busted Flush*. A flush is a sequence of cards in a poker game. He must be a gambler. This is characterization, woven seamlessly into the action, as is all the description. If you look at those two short paragraphs, virtually every sentence serves two purposes: (1) to show us what's going on; and (2) to acquaint us with the protagonist and his world. That's nifty writing.

You don't have to open your novel with action. But, to be on the safe side, try to choose something that provokes readers in some way, by making them ask questions, springing a surprise on them, or making them laugh.

Here are some examples:

- 'He semed incapable of creating such chaos, but much of what he saw below could be blamed on him' (*The Pelican Brief*, by John Grisham). Question: What chaos and what's he done to cause it?

- 'It was a bright cold day in April and the clocks were striking thirteen' (*Nineteen Eighty-Four*, by George Orwell). This is a surprise. Normal clocks don't strike thirteen.

- 'It can hardly be a coincidence that no language on Earth has ever produced the expression "as pretty as an airport" ' (*The Long Dark Tea-Time of the Soul*, by Douglas Adams). A shared joke: we warm to the author and the story to come.

Causality

E. M. Forster defined plot as a sequence of events, the emphasis falling on causality. For example. 'The king died and then the queen died' is not a plot because the two events, although a sequence, are not related. However, 'The king died and then the queen died of grief' *is* a plot, because the second event is caused by the first.

Without this causal element, no plot can work. It's like a car without wheels – going nowhere.

I think it helps to think of plot as a row of dominoes, in which each domino must justify its existence by having an effect on one that comes after it. Aristotle referred to this as plot *unity*. According to him, the various incidents in a plot 'must be so arranged that if any one of them is differently placed or taken away the effect of wholeness be seriously disrupted. For if the presence or absence of something makes no apparent difference, it is no real part of the whole.'

Many writers make the mistake of thinking that plot is

just a series of action-packed scenes. Not necessarily. A man once handed me a manuscript in which the main character, a sailor, was treated to a ride in a Harrier jump-jet. The author spent a whole chapter on this, describing everything in vivid detail.

Sadly, the incident had no dramatic purpose. Nothing happened as a result of the ride. The main character missed no important phone calls, gleaned no fresh information, discovered nothing about himself that he didn't already know. This made the scene irrelevant to the story and it should have been cut.

Nothing, no matter how exciting in itself, is plot if it doesn't have repercussions. The corollary to that is that even the most trivial incident, if it has significant consequences, is plot.

If you remember this, your story will have structure. To make it a story that people will enjoy reading, you need more.

Goals, needs, wishes and desires

Main characters must always be motivated if they're to move the plot forward. If your characters don't much care how the story turns out, the most exciting plot in the world will be about as taut as a dead chicken's neck.

For this reason, it's a good idea to identify early on what each main character wants; and why. Aristotle said: 'Man is his desire.' Your characters' actions will be determined by their needs. The stronger the drive, the more powerful your story. Wishy-washy motives have no place in fiction.

In mass-market literature, it's particularly important that the characters' objectives are clear and believable. If you put in something the readers can't fathom, they won't identify with your characters. Psychologists have identified certain primary wants which we all share, and which we are all driven to satisfy. These wants aren't equally strong in everybody, but they're still there, even if unconscious.

Want to know what they are? Here goes:

1 Bodily comfort
2 A sense of security/self-preservation
3 To escape
4 To appease anyone who has power to injure
5 To be (a) noticed (b) admired (c) liked, by
   others of one's kind
6 To overcome and dominate – to feel superior
7 To attract a mate
8 To look after and protect someone
9 The company and fellow-feeling of others of
   one's kind
10 To be like others of one's own 'pack', especially
   its leaders. This is the herd instinct
11 To catch and capture
12 To find out, to know, to understand
13 To return to familiar people, places and
   conditions.

You're probably thinking that these wants don't apply to everybody. Take number 6, for example: surely not everyone wants to feel superior. Oh, don't they? Every time we compete with others, whether it's a game of tennis, a promotion at work, or a cake-baking competition, isn't that exactly what we're doing?

If this need is frustrated, we may be driven to seek gratification in strange ways. There's an interesting story of a little boy who was hopeless at school and ignored at home. There seemed no way in which he could possibly satisfy his need. But he had one talent of which he was proud: he could spit farther than anyone else. P. G. Wodehouse created this sort of character for one of his books – a man whose only talent was that he could make the sound of a chicken as it laid an egg.

Similarly, take Number 11. This is the hunting instinct, but it's for you to decide whether your character's 'prey' is the biggest fish in the lake, a valuable painting or, like Indiana Jones's, the Ark of the Covenant.

Remember, these wants are primitive. It's how we *express* them and try to satisfy them that's of interest to writers. The same primary want may be responsible for a hundred or even a thousand different behaviour patterns.

Look at each of your characters, find a want that's not being met, give it expression, and you've got your plot moving in the right direction.

Opposition

Plots come into being when characters with needs or wants hit obstacles.

'If I wanted to write a novel that would sell, I would get some likeable characters and invent a situation that would try them almost beyond endurance. I would wish the reader to recognise himself in one of the characters and show how they won or lost according to their capabilities.'

Some good advice there from Paul Gallico, author of *The Poseidon Adventure*. The *Poseidon*, in case you don't know, is a fictional cruise liner overturned by a giant wave in the Atlantic ocean. It's a good old escape story (see number 3 in Primary Wants).

Your story may be very different from Gallico's but the principle he expounds is right on the button. If your characters just go ahead and satisfy their wants, you've not got much of a page-turner.

The answer is to create opposition, obstacles, complications, to foil your characters in their quest. The opposition could be in the form of a person, or people, whose wants clash with those of the main character. In Daphne du Maurier's *Rebecca*, for example, the heroine's desire to win her husband's love is blocked by the housekeeper, Mrs Danvers, who does her utmost to cause trouble. She has a motive, of course. She loved the hero's first wife and is jealous of the second.

It could be a series of natural or mechanical disasters. Thomas Hardy was fond of those. In *Far from the Madding Crowd*, Gabriel Oak's desire to marry Bathsheba is cruelly thwarted when his dog drives all his sheep over a cliff. And, as is typical of Thomas Hardy, the disasters keep coming, affecting each of the book's main characters in turn. Fire, storms, crop failure, illness among the animals. Each disaster plays its causal part, effecting change in both characters and the direction of the plot.

The opposition could also arise from within the main character. This comes in two flavours and we'll deal with them separately because they each produce a different effect.

1 Give your character flaws or attributes which make him his own worst enemy. For an example of literature's most self-destructive character, look at Hardy's *The Mayor of Casterbridge*. We already touched on this in Chapter Four when we discussed Michael Henchard's attempt at one-upmanship over Farfrae. But the fatal flaws surface at the beginning of the book. Henchard gets drunk at a village fair and, in a fit of pique, sells his wife to a passing sailor. Sober, he's appalled and takes a vow of abstinence for twenty-one years.

Henchard is not a bad man. We couldn't sympathize with him if he were. He keeps to his vow and makes a new life for himself. What makes him such a powerfully tragic figure is the continuous internal conflict between weakness and strength. When challenging the more puny Farfrae to a fight, for example, he insists on tying one of his own arms behind his back so as not to gain an unfair advantage.

Later, his return to drink after twenty-one years on the wagon leads to personal and public disgrace. Yet, when declared bankrupt, his honesty forces him to hand over his gold watch. If you're interested in seeing a character whose every action hurls him closer to a black hole, this is a good book to read.

Martin Amis's character John Self, in *Money*, is similarly doomed, although this book is a comedy. Self spends most of the time drinking himself into oblivion, being rude to everyone, spending money he doesn't have, and finally – by having a sexual romp with his old girlfriend – ruining his chances with a woman he cares about.

2 Give your character a conflict of interests. This is a writer's super-weapon because it generates tension of the highest calibre. When a character faces opposition from other people or from environment, the way forward is never in doubt. Defeat the antagonist, climb the mountain, or whatever. When your character is faced with internal conflict, there's no easy answer. It's a question of the devil and the deep blue sea.

Let's look at an example. In the climactic scene of the film *Sleeping With the Enemy*, Julia Roberts faces her wife-beating husband with a gun in her hand. As the victim of violence, she abhors it. If she pulls that trigger, she herself becomes a killer. She's also terrified. Her hands are shaking, and she knows that if she misses there'll be no second chance. Her husband will kill the man she now loves, and possibly her as well. What does she do?

Well, what would you do? This is what makes inner conflict so powerful. We, the readers, or in this case the audience, are forced to question our own belief system. The decision we make shows us what kind of person we ourselves are.

Julia Roberts pulls the trigger. She had a primary need: self-preservation.

When the motivating force is love, the situation becomes even more poignant.

When a dog starves to death rather than leave the body of his owner who has fallen into a mine-shaft, it touches our hearts.

When a mother from Sarajevo jettisons her own instinct for self-preservation and dies protecting her child (remember little Irma?) the world is moved.

When Hollywood lets a man like Humphrey Bogart sacrifice his own happiness for that of the woman he loves, it's on to a winner. *Casablanca* has become a cult movie. Its success owes a lot to the final scene in which Bogart makes Bergman go back to her husband. If you stay with me, he tells her, you'll regret it. And as he drawls those immortal words. '... maybe not today, maybe not tomorrow, but soon. And for the rest of your life,' all we can do is sigh and snivel into our Kleenexes.

This is the ultimate aim of all conflict, to involve the readers with the characters to the extent that they care passionately about the outcome of your story. As Brecht said, in one of his last poems:

> When I say what things are like
> Everyone's heart must be torn to shreds.

If you can achieve that, you too are on to a winner.

Conflict, crisis and change

OK, you've got your characters and you've given them worthy opposition. Now all you have to do is keep them batting at that opposition for the next 70,000 words. Right?

Wrong. That approach might work in a short story, but a novel is different. A novel isn't a hurdle race. It's a game in which the characters have to make choices, without always knowing whether that choice is the right one. It's a game in which the ratchet turns and there's no going back.

A lady who had written six unpublished novels asked me to read her latest one. It was a historical romance. The heroine wanted the hero. The hero's mother didn't want her to have him. The heroine was also trying to raise money to build some cottages for the poor. As I read, I started to have feelings of *déjà vu*. In one scene, someone objected to the cottages; in the next the heroine had won him over. In another scene, the hero's mother was awkward; in the next, the heroine had baked a cake and got back into favour.

The book didn't have a hope in hell of getting published. The conflict had three serious flaws:

1 Each problem existed in its own little vacuum. No problem affected the book as a whole.

2 The problems were solved too quickly and too easily.

3 The problems did not alter the *direction* of the story. Any one of them could have been rearranged or left out without the reader noticing. The result was like a flat road stretching into the distance with no twists or turns. There was no rising tension.

You probably don't need me to tell you that every book has a central conflict or problem that must remain unresolved until the final climax. This is the top of the mountain. To get there, the readers must feel as if they're climbing that mountain right along with the characters. If you've ever climbed a mountain, or even a steep hill, you know what it's like. You can't go in a straight line. Sometimes the path falls away and you have to shift sideways. You may even have to go back down a little way and choose a different path altogether. Occasionally, your feet will slip.

It's the same with a plot-line. The way to the top must be strewn with a series of mini-climaxes. If not, the reader will lose interest. Consequently, we need to build our internal scenes in three steps: conflict (in whatever form) leading to crisis leading to change. Change occurs when the problem either gets worse or forces the character on to a different path. If it does neither, the scene is nothing more than a delaying tactic.

Dean Koontz once gave the following example of a delaying tactic. A murder has been committed and the protagonist is a suspect. However, he has an alibi, a girl he spent the night with. He goes to her apartment, only to find that she's left for the airport. He calls a cab, reaches the airport just in time to see her plane taking off....

You get the idea? It's certainly conflict but the overall direction of the story hasn't changed.

Let's have another go. The main character goes to his lover's apartment and finds that she's dead.

See the difference? Before, to prove his innocence, all the hero had to do was find his lover. Now, he has to do a re-think. He must find the real murderer to prove he's been framed.

Not only have the stakes been raised, but the scene has radically altered the progression of the story.

This principle holds true for all fiction, not just thrillers or fast-action stories:

'You leave a cinema, but forget your raincoat. You go back and find in the next seat your future wife.' Alan Ayckbourn once gave that example of how a single moment can make our lives shift direction. It's a theme he explores in *Intimate Exchanges*, a permutation of stage plays, all stemming from the same initial scene in which a woman has to make a choice:

(1) Should she have her first cigarette of the day before six o'clock?

(2) Should she resist?

If she decides on (1) the play goes in one direction. If (2) it goes in another. Ayckbourn writes scenes for both. The play continues to divide, with each subsequent scene giving the characters further and more crucial choices of action, the consequences of which are all explored.

Intimate Exchanges has thirty different scenes, which can be permutated to make sixteen different versions of the play. It's a fascinating study of the thought processes involved in planning a plot. I suggest you read it.

Transitions

Transitions are the means by which we bridge gaps in time or space, getting our characters from a bar in Soho to a party in Fulham, jumping from the last week of April to the first of September, or switching from Ted in Teddington to Jane in the jacuzzi.

Transitions are easier for writers than they used to be because, thanks to television, we're now living in the age of the fast cut. In literature, it's more of an extra-line gap. Like this:

Gaps allow the writer to cut out what Susan Hill described as the 'chores' of writing. 'I simply do not have to do the chores, write the dull bits. I leave them out. Leave the reader to make huge leaps. And the best thing of all is that it works far, far better. It is boring to read a book in which we are made to plod anxiously all the way from A to B. Even more boring to write one. Hop, skip and jump, like Alice over the hedges between the chess squares. Simple.'

Well, it isn't always *that* simple. Suppose, for example, your main characters have just succeeded in escaping from the enemy (it doesn't matter who). After a nail-biting chase scene, they're now waiting at an isolated airstrip for the rescue plane. You, as writer, know that in a short while that plane is going to appear overhead. But what do you do with those few anxious minutes?

Well, you could leave a gap and start again with: 'Harry suddenly pointed a finger and said, "Hey, folks, see what I see?"' But this would look contrived.

On the other hand, if you have them all sitting around twiddling their thumbs, tension will drain like water through a sieve.

Alistair Maclean faced this precise problem in *Where Eagles Dare* when Major Smith and his party arrive at Oberhausen airfield. The author solved it quite simply by switching viewpoint to the pilot of the rescue plane. Now, instead of the fugitives waiting for the plane, the plane is looking for them. For the readers, this actually heightens the tension instead of draining it.

Another technique is the link. With this, you maintain continuity by carrying an element from one scene across to the next. A particularly nifty example occurs in *The Day of the Jackal*, in which the element is a line of dialogue spoken by one person in one office, and repeated later in another:

'The identity of the assassin must be revealed by a secret enquiry, he must be traced wherever he is, in France or abroad, and then destroyed without hesitation.'

'... and destroyed without hesitation.'

In the new scene, we immediately know what's being discussed because we heard it before.

The link doesn't have to be dialogue. It could be anything:

'Have you seen Neil lately?'

Miranda shook her head. 'He told me he was doing some charity work, but I don't know quite what.'

In the Blue Fox, Neil[1] leant against the bar and knocked back a whisky. Well, most of the whisky. Some of it splashed right out again because the left side of his mouth was still numb from the injection. Something had obviously gone badly wrong with his smile too, if the reaction of that woman in the silk dress was any guide.

The numbness[2] hadn't worn off when it was time to go and see Ellery. Neil didn't expect that to be a pleasant experience. It never was. But this was worse than most. Ellery didn't want to be killed. He was strong too, and when Neil shoved the gun against his spine, Ellery kind of jack-knifed and took a bullet through the head.

It was a mess. Neil imagined Ellery's Puerto Rican maid coming in tomorrow morning, expecting to polish a few mirrors, vacuum the carpet, switch on the dishwasher. Instead – this. Most of Neil's victims were found by their cleaners. Idly, he wondered if there was a support group for people who found their employers looking like a dogfood commercial. Then another idea occurred to him. Why not pay the cleaners to do his work for him?

He was still thinking about this[3] as, back in the car, he headed east on the interstate. Naah, the maids would get greedy and he'd just have to kill them. That would not be nice. Neil liked women and he could think of more pleasant ways of spending time with them. Rummaging in the glove compartment, he found a packet of cigarettes. At least he could clamp one of those between his teeth without fear of mishap.

Two chain-smoked cigarettes[4] later, he was standing in line at International Check-ins.

OK, so in an actual novel, we might not want Neil moving at quite such a lick, but you get the idea? The links here are: [1] a name, [2] a feeling, [3] a thought, and [4] a time substitute. Instead of the chain-smoked cigarettes, we could simply have said, *twenty minutes* later, but it's fun sometimes to think of alternatives.

11

Spiking the Mixture

When I teach writers' workshops, I hand out evaluation sheets at the final session. This is everyone's chance to tell me what they enjoyed most about the class (and what they didn't!). The first time I did this, one student wrote: 'I've been introduced to techniques I never knew existed.'

That's what this chapter is all about: special techniques. Unless you're just starting out, some will be familiar to you. Others may be new. Even if you can't immediately find a use for them, you'll know that they're there.

Symbolism

Something exciting is going to happen in your plot. You want to whet the readers' appetite without giving too much away. How do you do it? You have two options.

You can be clumsy: 'Had he known what awaited him, he might have thought twice about going out that night.'

Or you can be subtle. Symbolism is subtle because it allows us to adjust our readers' mood without them ever being aware of it. The following example comes from Robert Ludlum's *The Parsifal Mosaic*:

> The man in the dark overcoat and low-brimmed hat that shadowed his face climbed out of the two-toned coupé; with difficulty he avoided stepping into a wide puddle by the driver's door. The sounds of the night rain were everywhere, pinging off the hood and splattering against the glass of the windshield, thumping the vinyl roof and erupting in the myriad pools that had formed throughout the deserted parking area on the banks of the Potomac river.

On the surface, this is a straight descriptive passage and a pretty dull one at that. I mean, who cares about the sound of the rain? Take another look. The rain is 'pinging', 'splattering', 'thumping', 'erupting'. These are violent words and that's why they're there. The rain is a symbol of the mayhem to come: the bullets, the battery, the thud of bodies. On a subliminal level, the readers know this. As a result, their expectations are raised and their interest alerted.

Symbolism works because life itself is chock-full of it. TV commercials are an obvious example. Think of all those washing powder commercials featuring actors in white coats. White coats are worn by doctors, whom, for some strange reason, most of us trust. White itself is a symbol of purity. It's the stuff of wedding dresses, snow, and – yes – clean washing.

Other colours, too, have symbolic significance. See what you make of the following passage:

> There was a great crop of cherries at the farm. The trees at the back of the house, very large and tall, hung thick with scarlet and crimson drops, under the dark leaves. It had been a hot day and now the clouds were rolling in the sky, dark and warm. Paul climbed high in the tree, above the scarlet roofs of the buildings. The wind, moaning steadily, made the whole tree

rock with a subtle, thrilling motion that stirred the blood. The young man, perched insecurely in the slender branches, reached down the boughs where the scarlet beady cherries hung thick underneath, and tore off handful after handful of the sleek, cool-fleshed fruit. Cherries touched his ears and his neck as he stretched forward, their chill finger-tips sending a flash down his blood. All shades of red, from a golden vermilion to a rich crimson, glowed and met his eyes under the darkness of the leaves.

There are seven references to colour in this passage, all varying shades of red. It's a symbol, but of what? A student once suggested it could be war, a battle in which people were hurt and blood was spilled. That's not a bad idea. Certainly the passage is suffused with emotion: the wind 'moaning', the clouds 'dark and warm', the 'thrilling' motion of the tree.

But it's not war. The book is *Sons and Lovers* and, in context, this scene is a symbol of sexual passion. In the next paragraph, when Paul's girlfriend, Miriam, appears beneath the tree, the readers' mood is on course for what's going to happen.

Symbolism is a versatile technique. In the above examples, the descriptive passages set up expectations in the reader, which the author then fulfils. But symbols can be used whenever you want to convey something to the reader, or make a point, without being obvious. In George Orwell's *Nineteen Eighty-Four*, for example, the varicose ulcer on Winston Smith's leg is a symbol of his hidden unhappiness and isolation. During his love affair with Julia, the ulcer subsides to a brown stain, mirroring his inner joy. Later, when he's captured by the Thought Police, the return of this ulcer points up his pain.

Action, too, can be symbolic. If a woman who's always kept her hair up suddenly lets it down, the readers will know that changes are afoot. Similarly, if a man whose pride is his garden shows a sudden loss of interest, that behavioural switch will be seen as a mirror of internal flux.

Symbols add substance to your writing because they give the reader something to do. Novels in which everything is on the surface, where there are no little mysteries and nothing to interpret, are like bare fields.

An exercise in symbolism

Imagine that you are writing the first page of your novel. Using the D. H. Lawrence and Robert Ludlum extracts as a guide, create an atmospheric mood of your choice. Remember to use words and images that convey your purpose subtly, rather than making it a bald statement. Here are some ideas:

Romantic	Erotic
Mysterious	Violent
Supernatural	Jet-setting
Horrific	Homely

Student example

In the moonlight, the shadow from a huge bent oak tree claws at the house. Behind the windows, every blind is drawn – closed eye-lids in an expressionless face. Splitting the face is a porch covered in ivy, tendrils twisting and contorting.

A man walks towards the house, his long grey overcoat buttoned, his footsteps silent on the slimy leaves.

Judy Smith

Intertextuality

If ever there was a magic technique, this is it. You may remember we talked about the impossibility of being 'original'? With intertextuality, we deliberately choose ingredients that are tried and tested, narrative situations which provoke in the reader 'a sort of intense emotion accompanied by the vague feeling of *déjà vu* that everybody yearns to see again'.

That definition comes from Umberto Eco, who suggests that intertextuality is responsible for the success of many cult movies. He cites *Casablanca*, which he says is a hodge-podge of sensational scenes strung together implausibly, with characters who are psychologically incredible. Nevertheless, *Casablanca* is a persistently mesmeric film and is now used as the basis of a screenwriting course which runs in America and occasionally in London.

The source of its success is interesting. The screenwriters made up the plot as they went along. Even in the final scene, no one knew what was going to happen until the last moment. Forced to improvise, the writers threw in everything they could think of. Fortunately, it all came from a repertoire that had stood the test of time. *Casablanca* works because it's not *one* film.

It pulls in themes from myth and legend, war and intrigue. Similarly, the main character is a composite of irresistible hero 'types'. He is the tough guy from the gangster movie, the self-made businessman, the adventurer, the damaged lover who drinks to forget.

The technique that the screenwriters of *Casablanca* employed so artlessly is now used consciously by film makers like Steven Spielberg in the *Indiana Jones* films. When you watch these movies, you can see the echoes, the motifs that have the power to thrill us again and again.

Doesn't this sound like a recipe for cliché? It could be. I'm not suggesting that you simply plagiarise the last book you read, on the basis that what worked for that author will work for you too. The trick is to choose only those ingredients that are *guaranteed* to work, ones whose appeal is deeply rooted in the human psyche.

One author who has done this with great success is Joan

Aiken. In an article entitled 'How to Keep the Reader on the Edge of the Chair', she talks about tried and reliable threat situations and how she used them in her novel *The Wolves of Willoughby Chase*. Let's look at her opening:

> It was dusk – winter dusk. Snow lay white and shining over the pleated hills and icicles hung from the forest trees. Snow lay piled on the dark road across from Willoughby Wold, but from dawn men had been clearing it with brooms and shovels. There were hundreds of them at work, wrapped in sacking because of the bitter cold, and keeping together in groups for fear of the wolves, grown savage and reckless from hunger.

Bearing in mind that this is a children's story, what elements here might we see as intertextual? There are several:

- Wolves. Ever since *Little Red Riding Hood*, wolves have had a role as the baddies of children's stories.

- Forests. They appear in most traditional fairytales, and are associated with both danger and adventure.

- Snow. For children, snow is always magical, evoking images of Christmas and heightened emotion.

Later in the book, more irresistible elements appear: a secret passage; a wicked governess; a ghastly orphanage (echoes of Dickens), where children are half-starved and have their hair cut short (remember Jane Eyre?). The author also uses the device of an intercepted letter. The children smuggle out a letter asking for help, but it's discovered and destroyed. That, Aiken says, came from *Uncle Silas* by Sheridan Le Fanu. Whatever kind of novel you're writing, it's well worth doing a creative search for no-fail ingredients. To start you off, here are some scary ones:

- Villains. For some reason, physical irregularity, or disability, is very frightening in villains (the contrast between strength and weakness, perhaps?). *Treasure Island* gives us Blind Pew and Long John Silver. Mary Stewart has one of her villains confined to a wheelchair. Similarly, no one who's read *Jamaica Inn* could forget the evil albino posing as a clergyman.

Also on the shivers list are people wearing masks or clown costumes (see *It*, by Stephen King).

- Birds. Daphne du Maurier used real ones in *The Birds*. Stuffed ones can be even more menacing.

- Inanimate objects. Unlike humans, inanimate objects can't be reasoned with. That takes them into the realms of the unknown. Take dolls. *Maelstrom*, one of the most gripping TV thrillers I've ever seen, featured a house on an island in a Norwegian lake. Before she died, a woman had been using it as an artist's retreat. As the heroine walks alone through the deserted rooms, she finds hundreds of dolls, one with a real tear on its cold cheek. On an easel is a painting, clearly the work of a deranged mind.

What made this thriller so good was the combination of ingredients. Along with the dolls, we had mental instability and an isolated setting, all classic elements of suspense.

So why aren't they a cliché?

Because the author gave them each an original slant. The dolls were not one-eyed uglies, but were all dressed up in extravagant clothes. The mental instability was expressed, not with wild hair and screams, but subtly, through the paintings. The setting was not the traditional gothic mansion, but a pastel-pretty house on a silent lake.

An exercise in suspense

Take those same three elements of setting, madness and inanimate object(s). Do a creative search to find an original slant on each. Then, using the what if? technique mentioned in Chapter Ten, draft a plot-line for a super-scary story.

Integrated action and setting

One way of adding originality to our novels is to select actions and settings that are uniquely suited to both the plot and the characters. A classic example is *Wuthering Heights*, in which the brooding Yorkshire moors are the perfect backdrop for the passionate love between Cathy and the half-wild Heathcliff. By contrast, in many of Jane Austen's novels, the elegance of Bath mirrors the polite manners of the principal characters.

In John D. McDonald's Travis McGee series, the main character, McGee, is described as 'part rebel, part philosopher, and every inch his own man'. The crimes he gets to investigate are much the same as any other author's crimes. It's his setting that makes him different. He lives in Florida on a houseboat which he won in a poker game (now *that's* original), and many key scenes take place below deck. Where another sleuth might jump into a battered convertible, McGee simply casts off the lines and chugs around the waterways until he gets where he wants.

It's a good foil for the violence which erupts fairly often.

In the film *Witness*, Harrison Ford's character is a big-city cop, recuperating from a gunshot wound sustained while trying to protect Rachel, an Amish mother, and her son (the witness). For most of the film, the setting is the Amish community in Pennsylvania. In one sequence, the whole neighbourhood is involved in raising a barn. The men do the carpentry, the women hand out food. This is certainly action but, at first glance, you might wonder if the scenes are really significant.

Yes, they are. It's during this sequence that Harrison Ford

sees the Amish community as an intrinsic part of Rachel's life. He realizes, too, that he can never belong. Later, when he sees Rachel stripped to the waist, washing in the kitchen, he resists the temptation to become her lover. Instead, he knows he must leave.

That barn-raising sequence is a perfect example of integrated action. To appreciate it fully, you might like to ask yourself what other action the writer might have chosen to achieve that effect. What could have been more appropriate? It synchronizes with the characters. It suits the plot.

When choosing action for your novel, look at the particular qualities of your characters and their lives. If your characters are individuals, this shouldn't be difficult. See if you can come up with something unique, like that scene in *Witness*.

Foreshadowing

Anton Chekhov once said that if you're going to fire a gun in the third act, the audience must see it being loaded in the first. What he's saying is that events in fiction mustn't happen out of the blue, as if the author had just thought of them.

A bridge that was perfectly sound in Chapter Two can't suddenly collapse in Chapter Eight as the baddies drive over it. Sane characters can't suddenly become mad just because it suits our purpose. Dormant volcanoes can't suddenly erupt without first doing a little spitting and grumbling.

But surely an element of surprise is what keeps people reading? Yes. But there's a difference between being surprised and feeling cheated. Surprises must be planned or they'll appear like coincidences.

In real life, coincidence happens all the time. In fiction, it's a contrivance that makes the reader hopping mad. The reason is simple. Coincidence offers the writer an easy way out of any situation. It's like those games we used to play as children where the rules changed as we went along: 'Sorreee, can't catch me, I've just turned invisible' sort of thing.

The answer is to use foreshadowing, to insert a 'plant' whose significance is lost on the reader until later in the story. Let's look at an example.

In one of television's *Miss Marple* stories, various characters receive an anonymous invitation to a 'Murder'. The two ladies whose home is the venue seem as bemused as everyone else. Indeed, the hostess's main concern seems to be the central heating, which she has switched on in anticipation of a chilly evening. At the time, there's no way we can appreciate the significance of this. In the context of friendly greetings, it passes us by.

In fact, it's a 'plant'. In the final episode, that seemingly innocuous remark is produced by Miss Marple as evidence of guilt. The murderer needed darkness to commit the crime. That meant no fire in the grate. Without a fire, the central heating was needed. The only person in a position to control that was the hostess herself.

Obvious, isn't it? In retrospect, yes. In context, no. At the time, the hostess was the last person to be suspected. When the lights come up, she's sitting in a chair with blood on her shoulders. One of the bullets has apparently clipped her ear. It's a beautiful red herring.

'Plants' work because readers register what appears to be important and discard the rest – that's what we count on.

Time-shift

Most novels are written in the past tense, irrespective of their actual place in time. A science fiction story, for example, may be set in 2050, but it's unlikely to start: 'On a warm morning in 2050, Seth will pull on his jeans and plug in his brain'. An exception is Michael Frayn's *A Very Private Life*:

'Once upon a time there will be a little girl called Uncumber.' But Frayn can't keep it up and soon reverts to the present.

The present tense is not unusual. However, the past tense – 'Seth *pulled* on his jeans and *plugged* in his brain' – remains the favourite of most writers. Readers are aware of this. So, when they pick up a novel and see the past tense, they accept it as the 'here and now' of the story. Any deviation from this 'here and now' is known as time-shift, and must be made clear to the reader, either by a change of tense or some other signal.

In most novels, time-shifts are used to acquaint the readers with events that happened in the characters' pasts. These are usually naturalized as memories. A man hears a few bars of a song and is instantly whisked back to 1971, for example.

We can deal with these memories in two ways.

Exposition If you use narrative summary to *tell* readers about the past, that's exposition:

> As he listened to that music, Mark wondered if he was destined always to be the outsider. Even when he was sixteen, he was never one of the crowd. Like everyone else, he'd worn the uniform of the time: flares, tie-dyed tee-shirts and a few hippy beads. But he'd never really felt comfortable. His hair wasn't right for a start. It should have been long and straight, and parted in the centre. Instead, it was frizzy, more like a tangled ball of wool than a pair of sleek curtains.

Note the switch from past tense into pluperfect – 'he'd worn' instead of 'he wore'. Strictly speaking, we don't need to change tense here because 'when he was sixteen' signals the time-shift to the reader.

The problem with exposition is that it's a touch dull. It

lacks action and drama, the things readers value. In small doses, it's fine. In longer stretches, it distances the reader and drains tension.

Flashback If you dramatize past events, show them as a scene, that's flashback. Scenes are more vivid because of the visual quality. Two pages of waffle can never compete with the immediacy of a picture:

> Mark listened to that hard, pulsing beat. In 1971, when he was sixteen, it had been top of the charts. Billy had played it at his party, a night that hovered in Mark's subconscious like a scabby sore, just itching to be scratched. He scratched it now and saw a molten mass of bodies gyrating beneath a light dimmed by red fabric. The air was thick with incense, beer and girls' cheap perfume. Mark, wearing his new purple flares – which must look good because his mother had told him they were obscene – sauntered over to the stereo. He hoped he didn't smell. He'd put Brut under his arms and other strategic places, just in case.

I shan't go on. I don't know what happens to Mark. Maybe his flares split just as he sidles up to the girl of his dreams, maybe he's sick in her lap, maybe he skids on the kitchen floor and gets cheesecake in his frizzy hair. It doesn't matter. What matters is that by focusing on a specific scene, we've enabled the readers to share Mark's recollection. When we leave the flashback and return to the present, the readers will be more likely to understand and sympathize with his insecurities.

Don't get too fond of flashbacks. I know they're seductive, but used gratuitously they're as dangerous as the sea nymphs whose songs lured sailors to a rocky death. Some things to consider:

• Flashbacks are disruptive because they stop the forward

movement of a story. Readers will tolerate this if they're sufficiently interested in a character to care about his past. It's vital therefore to establish the character in the context of the main story before launching into flashback.

- A character's past is only relevant when it has a direct bearing on what's happening in the present. As the writer, you will (or should!) know a lot about your characters' life histories. Don't be tempted to reveal it all just because it's there.

- Flashbacks are never as dramatic as a scene set in the 'here and now'. They're over. The character lived to tell the tale. Inevitably, this lowers the suspense.

The rule of three

This is a strange little rule that has its roots in artistic pattern. Look at the traditional folk-tale. It's no accident that there were three little pigs, two of whom built their houses out of silly materials and fell prey to the wolf. The Rule of Three operates on many different levels. Stories are divided into beginnings, middles and ends; scenes into problem, crisis and dénouement. Similarly, there's an appealing aesthetic symmetry to events which happen in threes.

In practice, this means that when your main character tries to overcome an obstacle, he or she must always fail twice before succeeding. There's a good reason for this. If the character succeeded the first time, there'd be no tension. If he succeeded the second time, it would be too easy – the first failure would be seen as a fluke. The third time, we know he can fail and that builds suspense. When he actually succeeds, we feel he deserves to.

Remember, though, to vary the circumstances each time. Think of those old *Star Trek* episodes: uh-oh, there's something nasty on Gamma Seven. All that's left of the scouting party is a disembodied message: 'Captain, it's coming for us....'

That's failure number one. OK, says Captain Kirk, I'm going down. Needless to say, he, too, disappears like a ghost who's just heard there's a white-sheet sale starting on a distant planet.

Finally, Mr Spock, who's a touch cleverer than the rest of them, strides on to the transporter, having taken the precaution of altering the co-ordinates. He beams down half a mile to the west, thus avoiding the bouffant-haired aliens lurking in the entrance to a polystyrene cave.

It's all about as subtle as a joke fried egg, but don't knock it. It works.

Subplots

Not all novels contain subplots. In a short Mills & Boon-type romance, for example, there may be no room for a second plot-line. Take a look at your novel. Is it single or multiple viewpoint? If multiple, you're probably going to need subplots to deal with the individual experiences of each character, even when they're all involved in the same situation. Subplots have many uses. Let's take a look:

- To pace the story. Suspense stories often use subplots as a break from the excitement. You can't keep readers continually at fever-pitch. On the other hand, you can't risk letting their interest flag.

  For example, a terrorist has left a bomb in a hospital. It's due to go off at six o'clock and it's one o'clock now. Someone has to defuse it.

  Exciting as that may sound, you can't spend 80,000 words focusing on bomb-disposal. What you can do is to use the bomb-disposal as the main plot, the thread that holds the whole story together. You then pace it with subplots focusing on a selection of people whose lives are affected, both inside and outside the hospital. This will give that main plot-line a momentum it couldn't achieve on its own.

In the end, of course, the bomb is just a plot device. Stories are about people, and only by getting to know them and their circumstances can the readers care passionately what happens to them.

- To strengthen a main plot-line. Stories in which there is a single question of crisis – will the bomb be defused in time? Will Ben save the firm from bankruptcy? Will Fred manage to escape from the menacing heavies? – are often too predictable. The readers know that in the end everything will be resolved.

  What we need here is not so much a subplot, but a parallel plot-line or plot-lines to maintain the readers' interest.

  In Alistair Maclean's *Night Without End*, for example, an airliner crash-lands on the Greenland icecap. One plot centres on the survivors' trek across the freezing wastes to civilization. Exciting as this may be, it isn't enough. Maclean gives us a parallel plot-line in which someone is killing people. Everyone is a suspect, except the viewpoint character. As you can imagine, this notches up the tension.

- To make the story move faster. Subplots propel a reader through a book. With a selection of things to worry about, the book seems busier and time flies faster. One word of warning: make sure each subplot is interesting, or the readers may skip. The danger then is of them missing something vital.

- To kindle character interest in a multi-viewpoint story, particularly in the kind of novel in which a group of people start off as individuals and then are drawn together in a crisis situation.

  In Arthur Hailey's *Airport*, the main plot concerns a sabotaged jetliner trying to land on a runway blocked by another plane. For this to work, we must sympathize with the key people, but we don't have time to get to know them in the context of the main action. The author uses subplots to characterize them in advance. One focuses on a pregnant stewardess who wants the captain to marry her; another on an air-traffic controller whose nerves have caused a mid-air collision; a third deals with the expert whose job it is to move the snowbound plane; and so on.

Only when all these subplots are in place, does the main thread draw them together.

- To mirror or contrast later action in the story. If a character behaves in a particular way in a subplot, we can predict he may behave in a similar fashion in the main plot. The action in the subplot therefore acts as a mirror. Alternatively, he may act differently, in which case it's a contrast. That jumpy air-traffic controller, for example. Will his nerve hold out? The question adds suspense.

An exercise in subplots

Next time you finish a book containing subplots, take it apart. Write down the main plotline and list the subs. The main plotline, by the way, is always the one that endures to the end of the book. For each subplot, identify:

- Where it starts
- Where it finishes
- How many characters it involves
- Whether the characters are main, subsidiary or a mixture
- Its purpose in relation to the book as a whole (mirror, contrast, pacing or whatever)
- How the author has woven it in. For example, does it last for ten pages and then die? Or is it threaded throughout the book, as an integral strand?

12

Sticky Bits and Endings

The first time your plot skids to a halt, it's scary, like hitting a patch of ice in your car and ending up on the pavement, two inches from a lamp-post. Last week, you had ideas falling out of your sleeves. This week – it's probably a Monday – you're beginning to wonder whether you're a writer at all. Maybe you should just trash the whole thing and take up origami?

We all feel like this from time to time. It's a good thing. When you think about it, writing fiction – believing that people will buy something we just made up – takes amazing arrogance. If we didn't have these little rushes of self-doubt, we'd be insufferable. Some of us are, of course, but let's not get into that.

It could be that you've just been trying too hard to get things right. If so, relax. Take a break. Have a drink. Sci-fi writer Anne McCaffrey says that when she gets writer's block she leaves what she's doing and goes for a ride on her horse: 'The important thing is to get away from it, and later find out where and when you went up the wrong path.'

Hemingway relied on his subconscious brain: 'I learned not to think about anything I was writing from the time I stopped writing until I started again the next day. That way my subconscious would be working on it and at the same time I would be listening to other people and noticing everything, I hoped; learning, I hoped; and I would read so that I would not think about my work and make myself impotent to do it.'

At the time he wrote this, Hemingway was living in Paris and had acquired the habit of dropping in on his friend Gertrude Stein. If you don't have a friend who writes, try to find one. There are things that only writers understand and it helps to share. Sometimes, just talking to someone who knows what you're feeling will soothe you enough to get you going once more.

If your main problem is simply getting down to work, you might like to do what John Steinbeck did while writing *East of Eden*. Every day, he wrote a letter to a friend, not to put in the post, but to get 'my mental arm in shape to pitch a good game'. Each letter was a preliminary exercise, a warm-up for the real writing of the day.

I'm a great believer in five-minute warm-ups. Not only do they pump up your creative muscle, but they can help clear your mind. OK, so maybe you just broke up with someone you love. You're not the first person who had to carry on writing when feeling upset. American author Laurence Block had written two-thirds of an adventure novel when his marriage collapsed. He had to finish the novel while living in a bed-and-breakfast.

When the book was published, he was surprised to find that even he couldn't determine where the break had come: 'There was no seam. My life had a seam in it, all right, that was a long time smoothing out, but the book was all of a piece from first page to last.'

William Burroughs said: 'Writing's an important way of living.' It's true. I've always found that the people who get most discouraged when things go wrong are always the ones who regard writing as something to do in their spare time. To be successful, you need the strength of knowing that writing is an integral part of your life – whatever.

Of course you'll hit problems. Who doesn't? A publisher once wrote to Rudyard Kipling: 'I'm sorry, Mr Kipling but you really don't know how to use the English language.' Dean Koontz got seventy-five rejection slips before his first sale; John Creasy got five hundred.

Feeling better? Good. Let's now have a look at some practical ways to unblock your plot.

Go back to character

A student who'd begun work on four novels told me he'd lost interest in them all around Chapter Three. Having read some of his work, I wasn't surprised. Instead of developing just one or two viewpoint characters, he'd tried to reveal what everyone was thinking. The result was a shallow, fragmented story in which no one – not even the writer – could really get involved.

If you're having trouble with your plot, it could be that your problem is really character. Forgive me for quoting the old adage, 'Character is Plot', but it really is true that strong characters and the conflicts between them are the basis of successful fiction. If you don't know enough about your characters, you can't write plots that exploit their strengths and weaknesses.

Biographical checklists

This is a good time to compile a biographical checklist for each main character. What are the character's favourite foods, their hang-ups, their attitude to money, their sexual history? These details may be totally irrelevant to your story, but that's not the point. What you're trying to do here is to get to know each character on several different levels. Just one of those levels may open up ideas.

When Lois Duncan began her teenage suspense novel *Stranger With My Face*, the hero was a conventionally handsome boy. Half-way through, she realized she needed to make him more interesting. But how? The answer she hit on was to give him a scarred face.

It's such a simple little change, but I promise you it worked. The emotional damage caused by this disfigurement was reflected in his personality, making him the kind of loner who would listen to the heroine's fears instead of dismissing them.

Scars, of course, can be mental as well as physical. By the time we reach adulthood, we're all damaged. The only question is: how? You might like to try a creative search for each character's scars. They may give you just the insight you need to get that plot moving.

Six ways to proceed

Remember *Intimate Exchanges*, the play with sixteen different versions? Use the same approach for your own plot difficulties. First, write down the situation that's giving you a headache. Then, without bothering to think too hard, list at least six ways in which the plot might continue.

It's important to write down *everything* that comes into your head, however silly or illogical. Open-mindedness and uninhibited thinking are key elements in any kind of creative thought. As Peter Evans and Geoff Deehan point out in *The Keys to Creativity*, one of the biggest blocks is the tendency to censor ideas before giving them a chance. The real world is full of brilliant notions that very nearly didn't make it because someone dismissed them as stupid. I always think of the man who invented nylon tights – he was told they'd never catch on because women needed stockings and suspenders to stop their girdles riding up.

A good way to overcome this Oh-no-that-wouldn't-work kind of block is to separate the idea from its evaluation. Simply put down everything you can think of and worry later about the practicalities.

Learn to think the impossible

Aristotle said that probable *impossibilities* were preferable to improbable *possibilities*. Locked-room mysteries are excellent examples of this principle in action. Even if you're not interested in writing a mystery, just reading one or two of these stories will give your mind a good stretch.

The best-known author of locked-room mysteries is John Dickson Carr who wrote dozens, all featuring an 'impossible' crime. Here, for example, is the blurb from *The Hollow Man* (also known as *The Three Coffins*):

> Two murders are committed in such a fashion that the murderer must not only have been invisible – but lighter than air. According to the evidence, this person killed his first victim and literally vanished, and then struck again in the middle of an empty street – with watchers at either end who saw nothing and no footprints in the snow.

Intriguing, isn't it? And the solution is not a disappointment. You may find a few John Dickson Carr mysteries in your local library. Failing that, Murder One bookshop in Charing Cross Road, London, has a good selection.

Still on the locked-room theme, the following little poser comes from 'Proof of Guilt', by Bill Pronzoni, first published in *Ellery Queen's Mystery Magazine*. To paraphrase:

A man receives a visitor in his office, which is on the sixteenth floor. When two witnesses hear a shot, they immediately lock the office door and call the police. The police find the man and his visitor alone in the room. The man has been shot dead. Although the police search the visitor, the office and the grounds below, they can't find the weapon. Yet the man did die of a gunshot. What's the solution?

When I offer this problem to writers' workshops I encourage everyone to be as silly as they like. They usually oblige. One student suggested tying the gun to a balloon filled with helium and simply popping it out the window. That's good and might work. Other suggestions include: guns disguised as exploding cigars (makes a change from egg on the face), guns hidden under toupées, guns made of rice paper which the murderer then ate. What preposterous ideas.

In fact, that last suggestion is pretty close to the truth. No, the gun wasn't made of rice paper but it did come apart and the murderer did eat it. He'd had plenty of practice as a metal-eater in carnival sideshows.

You see what I'm saying? Although the idea looks silly at first, it needs only slight modification to make it work. But you can't modify something if you've already dismissed it. Next time you have a plot problem, try the 'silly' approach. It may lead you to gold.

Throw in a curve

Real life is full of curves. One happened to me recently. I'd planned a trip to America. I had my ticket confirmed, my clothes ironed, my favourite shoes repaired, my hair cut. It was two days before the flight. What could possibly go wrong?

My passport. It had expired. As I stood staring down at it, all I could think was: why the hell didn't someone send me a reminder?

In fiction, a curve is anything that takes your protagonist by surprise. Such problems usually have an external source, in that the protagonist has no hand in them. Suppose two people who own an art gallery have a row. If one subsequently disappears, having drained the joint account, that's a problem, but it's not external because it arose from the row.

If, on the other hand, the two partners argue over where to hang a new painting, only to find that a burst pipe has flooded the gallery and destroyed everything, *that's* external.

All forms of natural disaster, from a change in the weather to fire and earthquake, fall into this category. In *The Thornbirds*, a fire caused by a lightning bolt rages through Drogheda, destroying 25,000 sheep. In *Gone with the Wind*, the burning of Atlanta is a man-made catastrophe, but it's still an external problem with which the characters must deal.

Creative search will help you dream up ideas to throw your characters off-course. The trick is always to make sure that the event, though unexpected, is not implausible. In Anya Seton's *Foxfire*, for example, the hero is an American hard-rock miner who loses his job after an explosion for which he's held responsible. As a result, he is free to accompany the heroine on her search for hidden gold.

Sounds a touch too convenient, right? In context it works, because the author establishes well in advance that someone holds a grudge against the hero and wants to destroy him. When he narrowly escapes death, the job loss appears an inevitable consequence, rather than coincidence.

Think of throwing your characters a curve whenever the plot needs juicing up. Raymond Chandler once said that, when the plot sticks, have two guys come through the door with guns. If you read his stories, it appears that Chandler's plots got stuck pretty regularly. but, as his success proves, the technique seems to work.

Write through your blocks

Stravinsky, once said, 'Do not despise the fingers, the fingers are great inspirers.' He was talking about music, but the same applies to writing.

Poet Craig Raine believes that if you sit down *every* day and just write, you'll get more ideas than if you just sit around waiting for the muse: 'It seems to me that the whole process of writing is being on the job. All the real inspiration takes place on the page.'

James Herbert is another writer who doesn't plan his books from start to finish. Although he has no problem coming up with good ideas, he admits that 'Getting stuck two-thirds of the way through is awful. I call it the pain barrier and just have to force myself to work through it.'

This is, of course, the romantic approach and, from personal experience, I know that it works. I even use it when I'm teaching. For example, I no longer plan my lectures before sitting down to write them. I know that if I waffle for half a page, a direction will come to me and off I'll go.

Of course, there's always the risk that you'll end up with junk. But does that matter if the alternative is a blank page? Give it a try.

Visualize the situation

Writers who eschew outlines will often say that they need to feel the novel unfolding as they write, to experience the situations with the same wonder and surprise as their characters.

As we saw in Chapter Ten, this isn't an approach that suits everybody. However, there's no doubt that when you're in the mind of your viewpoint character, sharing his or her thinking, you can see plotting possibilities that might elude you in an outline.

In an article entitled 'Building Without Blueprints', Tony Hillerman talks about a scene in which his protagonist is trapped in an empty State Capitol building. 'Before I began writing this section, I had no luck at all coming up with an idea of how I could allow him to escape.... Now, inside these spooky, echoing halls, I think as my frightened character would think, inspired by his terror.'

The frightened character tries a few locked doors before discovering the janitor's supply room. In here are fuse boxes and a gallon jug of liquid detergent. Having cut off the power, he runs off down the corridor, dribbling slippery detergent behind him.

Hillerman makes the point that in an outline he'd never have thought of that supply room or the detergent. Yet that's what makes the hero's escape both possible and plausible.

Even if you use creative visualization for nothing else, try it for plot problems. You'll find it pays dividends.

Making your exit

If you've been working from an outline, you've probably always known how your novel will end. On the other hand, you may have hit the last chapter and not have a clue. Don't worry. In her third book, *Kick a Tin Can*, Dianne Doubtfire didn't know the ending until the last page but one. Jeffrey Archer is the same: 'If I knew, you'd know. I only know the first two or three pages, then I pray.'

One writer who dodged the question altogether was John Fowles. *The French Lieutenant's Woman* has three possible endings, one happy, one sad and one simply vexing.

Call me finicky, but the whole idea of multiple endings seems to me to be a betrayal of the trust between author and reader. John Fowles got away with it because he's John Fowles. That doesn't make it a good idea.

A fitting end

What *is* a good idea is to try out different endings in your head. Choose the one that fits the story you've written. Endings, remember are an integral part of the whole novel. If this means changing the ending that appears in your outline, that's OK. You know your characters better now. Go with your instincts.

David Lodge's *Changing Places*, for example, is a book written in a variety of styles. The author did this deliberately to add interest to what he describes as a 'predictable' plot. In keeping with this mix of styles, the final chapter is written as a film script. Here's how it ends:

> 'PHILIP shrugs. The camera stops, freezing him in mid-gesture.'

It's an unusual finish and it works, but only because it fits in with the overall concept. It isn't something clever that the author just thought of.

Another technique is to make your ending mirror the beginning:

> 'They used to hang men at Four Turnings in the old days.
> 'Not any more though.'

These are the first two sentences of Daphne du Maurier's *My Cousin Rachel*. The last two sentences are identical. The author has brought us full circle. Technically, this is a time-shift story. The novel starts in the present, whizzes back to the past, and finally returns us to the present on the last page. At first sight, the main story appears to be a flashback, but it's more accurate to describe the beginning and ending as flashforwards, or a frame.

The frame is a popular structure. The beginning allows the writer to drop tantalizing hints about the story to come. And once the story is over, the flashforward ending ties a neat final bow.

In *My Cousin Rachel*, the final flashforward is only two lines. That's appropriate because it's not there as explanation. Those two lines are an echo. When we first hear them, spoken by the first-person narrator, we're not aware of how they fit. By the end of the story, their significance is clear.

Martin Amis's *Money* uses the same structure, but in a different form. The two flashforwards are addressed directly to the reader, 'the dear, the gentle' as Amis calls us. The first is a suicide note dated September 1981. It peaks our curiosity. The last is another rather longer note, dated December, January, 1981, 1982. Its effect is that of a PS in a letter.

Frames give stories a rather pleasing circularity. They're a modern version of the old prologue and epilogue. However, treat them with caution, particularly the ending, which should never be used as an excuse to tie up the threads of an untidy plot. In *Money*, we read the final note because we want to find out what happened about the suicide. Did he, or didn't he?

Without this unanswered question, the note wouldn't work.

Happy or sad?

Writing is power. With power comes responsibility. If your readers have stayed with you until the end of the book, they're now vulnerable. They'll feel close to the main characters, even to the extent of loving them like real people.

If you were finishing a love affair, you'd be gentle, wouldn't you? Even if you wouldn't, even if you're the cruellest person since the Marquis de Sade, think twice before indulging yourself at your readers' expense. You do, after all, want them to buy your next book. It may seem a great wheeze to have everyone die of food poisoning on the last page, but, unless your name is Shakespeare, be very careful.

It can be done. Kingsley Amis killed off his whole cast in

Ending Up, but the book is a black comedy and the reader knows it.

I'm not suggesting that your characters must always amble off into a blood-orange sunset. The contrived happy ending is as dishonest as the contrived sad one. However, if you're writing a genre novel, good must always triumph over evil, even if it doesn't manage to laugh in its face. With short romances, too, it's not sensible to make the hero's last words, 'Sorry, darling, you're wonderful in bed, but I'm marrying Myra because she bakes a good chocolate cake.'

Let the readers be your guide. What are their expectations? Aim to leave them feeling satisfied, accepting that the ending is the right ending, the only possible ending for that particular story. I think Richard Walter defined the feeling well when he talked about movies: 'Each viewer should be reminded of his own sweet and sour humanity. There should arise within each member a sense that what has transpired on the screen is really about him.'

Involve the main characters

In a multi-viewpoint story, you may be tempted to tie up a subplot involving lesser characters after the main climax. Don't. Once the main plot is over, all that's left is anticlimax. Save your big guns for the end.

Beware the long goodbye

I used to live next door to a couple of party animals. Every Saturday night, guests would leave at two in the morning and spend at least ten minutes in the driveway saying goodbye (I imagine this was a repeat of the last ten minutes inside the house). Once they'd climbed into their cars, there'd be another round of goodbyes, followed by a final blast on the horn as they pulled away.

In fiction, prolonged endings are boring. Don't forget

that, unlike movie audiences, readers can see the end coming. When that final page is turned, they mentally prepare themselves. Don't send your characters into a slow fade. Let them finish as they began, doing something, thinking something, living their lives:

> ... Was he going to see policemen waiting for him on every pier that he ever approached? In Alexandria? Istanbul? Bombay? Rio? No use thinking about that. He pulled his shoulders back. No use spoiling his trip worrying about imaginary policemen. Even if there *were* policemen on the pier, it wouldn't necessarily mean–
>
> '*A donda, a donda?*' the taxi driver was saying, trying to speak Italian for him.
>
> 'To a hotel, please,' Tom said. '*Il meglio albergo. Il meglio, il meglio!*'

These are the final paragraphs of *The Talented Mr Ripley*, by Patricia Highsmith. The book ends, as it begins, in the middle of things or, as the Romans used to say, *in medias res*. Notice the question 'Was he going to see policemen waiting for him on every pier?' This, combined with the action and dialogue, encourages the reader to look ahead. There's no doubt here that the character lives on beyond the pages of the book.

It makes sense to create ongoing characters, or at least characters with the potential to live another tale. If your book sells well, you'll want to write another – fast. And it's easier to do this with characters you know.

Ms Highsmith did exactly this; there are several books featuring the intrepid Tom Ripley.

Although series characters are most commonly found in detective fiction, many mainstream authors have realized the advantage of sequels and trilogies. Think of Edna O'Brien's *Country Girls*, Tom Sharpe's *Wilt*, Barbara Taylor Bradford's *Emma Harte*.

In the amusing finale to *The Hitchhiker's Guide to the Galaxy*, Douglas Adams even goes so far as to mention the title of the sequel. In this scene, Arthur has gone to bed with a copy of the above-mentioned guide and comes across the following entry:

> It said: '*The History of every major Galactic Civilization tends to pass through three distinct and recognizable phases, those of Survival, Inquiry and Sophistication, otherwise known as the How, Why and Where phases.*
>
> '*For instance, the first phase is characterized by the question* How can we eat? *the second by the question* Why do we eat? *and the third by the question* Where shall we have lunch?'
>
> He got no further before the ship's intercom buzzed into life.
>
> 'Hey, Earthman? You hungry, kid?' said Zaphod's voice.
>
> 'Er, well, yes a little peckish, I suppose,' said Arthur.
>
> 'OK, baby, hold tight,' said Zaphod. 'We'll take in a quick bite at the Restaurant at the End of the Universe.'

The Restaurant at the End of the Universe, is, of course, the title of the sequel.

Finally:

An exercise in sticky bits and endings

Have you ever set your video to record a film, only to find, when you finally get to watch it, that things were running late or the tape ran out, and you've lost the ending? This happens to me a lot. As a result, I have to guess a lot of endings. Only later do I find out if I'm right.

If you think about it, guessing the endings of stories that have already been written is plotting with a safety net, because there *is* a right answer. And you know what I've discovered? The more you practise, the better you get. It's a bit like doing cryptic crossword puzzles. If you're not used to them, they're difficult, but after a while, your mind gets into gear and you start to think as the compiler did.

You can, of course, do this exercise with a book, but I recommend you try a video first. The advantage of videos is that even with a full-length film you get the whole story in less than two hours. Thrillers like *Presumed Innocent* are good, as are episodes of detective series such as *Murder, She Wrote*. Remember to check the running length of the material so you can stop it before the dénouement. Then, fetch a piece of paper and jot down all the possible conclusions, with a justification for each.

If you want to do the same thing with a book, choose an author whose plotting skill you envy. I recommend Alistair Maclean because his structure is so perfect. You can also stop at the ends of chapters and ask: what's going to happen next? Then read on and see how your version differs.

Even if you're the world's worst plotter, this simple little exercise (practised regularly!) will shift the rust from your thought processes and get things moving. After a while, you'll find yourself looking ahead and making calculated guesses from the very beginning. As a result, you may even find yourself a little disappointed in your favourite authors. If that happens, rejoice. It means your own plotting is getting better.

13

The First Draft is Finished

Checklist for rewriting

Once you've finished your first draft, you can feel pretty proud of yourself. You stayed the distance. Now, it's time to cool down. Put your manuscript away for a couple of weeks. Next time you pick it up, you want to be able to look at it with the detached and critical eyes of a reader, meeting your characters for the first time. You can't do this until you've backed off a little.

TWO WEEKS LATER ... How're you doing? If you wrote your novel on a computer, now's the time to print it all out. Yes, it'll take forever, but you see things on paper that you miss on the screen.

Check your structure

Every successful novel has a central thread, or purpose, which holds it together. As a test of your novel, try to summarize this purpose in a single sentence.

In light, mass-market novels, where the reader isn't

expected to search for deeper meanings, this central purpose can usually be expressed in terms of the main character's goal or goals.

If you find this difficult, practise on your favourite films (films are often easier than books because they're less complicated.) For example, in both *Terminator* films, the central purpose is for the goodies to destroy the evil Terminator before he destroys them and the world they're protecting.

In a literary novel, where a fast plot is secondary to character interaction, this purpose may not be as obvious. But if it isn't there at all, if all you have is a bunch of characters mooching around, neither learning nor changing, the reader might reasonably ask: So what?

The object of a novel is to enlarge experience, not to convey facts. And since fiction is about people, the novel that satisfies is the one that delves into the essential nature of man and woman. By the end of your novel, the readers should have a fresh vision of the human condition, an insight into the conflicts arising from rivalry, love, ambition or whatever.

One way of getting your purpose into focus is to reduce your plot to a premise. The premise should include the basic facts about the characters, conflict and resolution. The premise for *Romeo and Juliet*, for example, could be: forbidden love can lead to tragedy. Here we see the characters: the lovers. We see the conflict: the love is forbidden. And we see the resolution: tragedy.

A successful premise must contain all three elements. 'If at first you don't succeed, try again', for example, is not a premise because it says nothing about the resolution. Better to say, 'The person determined to win will overcome amazing odds.' Similarly, 'Jealousy can poison a loving marriage,' or 'Selfishness leads to isolation.'

One step leads to another

Once you've established your novel's central purpose, do a step-outline of the whole novel. Mark your text every time something significant happens. This could be in the form of action, dialogue or internal monologue. What matters is that it contributes to the forward movement of the story. On a separate sheet of paper, record each happening in a few brief words.

For example, here is a step-outline of the first chapter of *Pride and Prejudice*:

• Dialogue between Mr and Mrs Bennet reveals that Mr Bingley, a rich single man has moved into the neighbourhood.

• Mrs Bennet's talk reveals a woman determined to see her daughters married.

• To this end, she persuades her husband to call on Mr Bingley.

A step-outline will help you in several ways. Firstly, you'll find it easier to identify patches of irrelevance that need to be cut.

Secondly, by looking at the gaps between marks, you'll see where the pacing needs fixing. A long stretch with nothing significant will slow down your story. You might want to cut, or transfer a bit of action from somewhere else.

Thirdly, you'll see if each movement advances the story in a steadily upward direction towards the final climax. If not, revise until it does.

Once you've got the framework of the book in order, it's time to look at more specific areas. Keep the following checklist nearby as you read through your typescript. It isn't a step-by-step guide because writing isn't a step-by-step process. It's more like juggling. Everything interacts.

Essential checklist

- Does your story start in the right place? Neither too soon, nor too late?

- Is your first chapter unputdownable? If it isn't, no agent or publisher will even pick up the second.

- Look at individual scenes. Does each have a structure, a mini-purpose?

- Does each chapter end on a tantalizing note?

- If you have flashbacks, are they both necessary and vivid?

- Have you prepared the reader for surprises by putting in foreshadowing?

- Have you checked for inaccuracies? We can all be caught out. Edgar Rice Burroughs put tigers into an early *Tarzan* book. (There are no tigers in Africa.) Similarly, don't have a coffee shop at one end of the town in one scene and somewhere else in another. If necessary, draw a map. Margaret Mitchell made a scale model of Atlanta for *Gone with the Wind*.

- Are your characters believable and consistent?

- Is the protagonist someone whom the reader can like, respect, or at least relate to?

- Do the main characters have sufficient motive for getting involved in the story? If their motive is trivial, the readers won't care if they win or lose. Remember, we're talking about the characters' motive, not yours.

- Do you have the right number of characters? Do they all pay their way? If you have some bit-part players, could you blend them into one person?

- Have you given the protagonists plenty of difficult problems which they must overcome?

- In facing their problems, do the protagonists discover a truth of which they were previously unaware? Do they learn something about themselves and emerge as better people?

- Are the characters' names right for them? Do they convey the right image? According to a survey in *Company* magazine, names have strange powers. Alan, for example, was seen as boring, Adam as ferociously intelligent, and Simon very attractive and quite bright. For girls, Kate, Emma and Sarah were universally adored, whereas Tracy was rated as possibly the most unintelligent woman to walk the face of the earth. (I won't tell you what Margret was.)

  Check that no two characters have similar names; that is, names beginning with the same initial letter, or containing the same vowels. Bill and Bob will lead to confusion. As will Jenny and Penny.

- Do you have a sufficient variety and contrast of characters?

- Check continuity in characters' appearance. I once read a novel in which the hero walked into the room wearing a suit and tie. Three pages later, he removed his jacket to reveal – a polo-neck jersey.

- Do characters all have their own unique voices?

- Does your dialogue sound natural?

- Check viewpoints. Are the right characters telling the story? Are there any unintentional switches?

- Search for gratuitous detail. Aristotle said that every line should do at least one of three things: define character, advance plot or create atmosphere. If it doesn't, prune it out.

- Have you translated the story into vivid scenes so the readers can visualize what's going on? According to one publishing director, 'The commonest mistake authors make is to tell you things rather than showing you – pages of exposition with no characters which yank you out of the book into the author's study.'

- Have you used the five senses to bring your scenes to life and to help your readers identify with your viewpoint character?
- Do you have a variety of interesting settings?
- Check for favourite phrases and words that crop up too frequently. Cut out and replace.
- Check lengths of paragraphs. Split up ones that go on too long.

Is it all worth it? Of course it is. Remember, the next person to read your work is an agent or publisher. When that manuscript arrives, it's got to impress. At the very least, it must look as if you know what you're doing.

What do publishers want? Well, markets change and genres vary, but the elements of good story-telling go on forever. In an interview with *Writers News*, Susan Watt, editorial director of Michael Joseph, said that she has the same requirements for a popular novel as she has for a literary one:

- The characters must ring true
- The readers must be able to understand them and their relationships
- The main character must be sympathetic
- The novel must have a good pace
- There must be a variety of scenes.

Diane Pearson, editorial director of Transworld, says that a good novel should grab – and hold – the attention: 'Sometimes a manuscript starts off terribly well and I get very excited but it collapses halfway through.' She suggests that new novelists should find their own style by doing masses of reading.

Finally, I asked agent Jane Judd if she could tell me the main reasons for manuscript rejection. Here's what she said:

> It could be very obvious problems like grammar, syntax, punctuation, in which case you probably wouldn't read more than a few pages. Some MSS are quite well presented and well written but suffer from being too derivative, lacking in imagination – a lot of writers don't seem to realize that you can write to a particular genre or form without resorting to clichés and stereotypes. Another problem is that the characters are not well-developed so they never come alive, and some writers have real difficulty with descriptive passages.

Imaginative writing, colourful characters, vivid settings. These are what we all want from a novel, aren't they? Provide them for your readers and you've got a success.

Bibliography

Non-fiction

Block, Lawrence: *Telling Lies for Fun and Profit* (William Morrow, USA)

Boylan, Clare (ed.): *The Agony and the Ego, The Art and Strategy of Fiction Writing Explored* (Penguin)

Braine, John: *Writing a Novel* (Methuen)

Brande, Dorothea: *Becoming a Writer* (Macmillan)

Burack, Sylvia K. (ed.): *How to Write and Sell Mystery Fiction* (The Writer, Inc., USA)

Egri, Lajos: *The Art of Creative Writing* (Citadel)

Evans, Peter, and Deehan, Geoff: *The Keys to Creativity* (Grafton)

Falk, Kathryn: *How to Write a Romance and Get it Published* (Penguin, USA)

Gardiner, Dorothy, and Walker, Kathrine Sorley (eds.): *Raymond Chandler Speaking* (Hamish Hamilton)

Gawain, Shakti: *Creative Visualization* (New World Library, USA)

Goldberg, Natalie: *Writing Down the Bones* (Shambhala, USA)

Harary, Keith, and Weintraub, Pamela: *Lucid Dreams in 30 Days* (The Aquarian Press)

Hildick, Wallace: *Children and Fiction* (Evans Brothers Ltd)

Mander, A. E.: *Psychology For Everyman (And Woman)* (Watts & Co)

Mullan, Bob: *The Enid Blyton Story* (Boxtree)

Nash, Walter: *Language in Popular Fiction* (Routledge)

Nell, Victor: *Lost in a Book: The Psychology of Reading for Pleasure* (Yale University Press)

Paice, Eric: *The Way to Write for Television* (Elm Tree Books)
Radway, Janice: *Reading the Romance: Women, Patriarchy and Popular Literature* (University of North Carolina Press)
Storr, Anthony: *Churchill's Black Dog and Other Phenomena of the Human Mind* (Fontana)
Symonds, Julian: *Bloody Murder* (Papermac)
Tobias, Ronald B.: *20 Master Plots* (Piatkus)
Walter, Richard: *Screenwriting* (Penguin, USA)
Wibberley, Mary: *To Writers with Love* (Buchan & Enwright)
Zuckerman, Albert: *Writing the Blockbuster Novel* (Little, Brown)

Fiction

Adams, Douglas: *The Hitchhiker's Guide to the Galaxy* (Weidenfeld & Nicolson)
　The Long Dark Tea-Time of the Soul (Heinemann)
Aiken, Joan: *The Wolves of Willoughby Chase* (Jonathan Cape)
Amis, Kingsley: *Ending Up* (Century Hutchinson)
　Lucky Jim (Victor Gollancz)
　The Old Devils (Jonathan Cape)
Amis, Martin: *Money* (Jonathan Cape)
　The Rachel Papers (Jonathan Cape)
Austen, Jane: *Pride and Prejudice* (HarperCollins)
Ayckbourn, Alan: *Intimate Exchanges* (Samuel French)
Bennett, Alan: *Talking Heads* (BBC Books)
Bingham, Charlotte: *Country Life* (Michael Joseph)
Bradbury, Malcolm: *The History Man* (Arrow)
Bradbury, Ray: *Dandelion Wine* (Hart-Davies)
　The Stories of Ray Bradbury (Granada Publishing)
Braine, John: *Room at the Top* (Eyre & Spottiswoode)
Brontë, Emily: *Wuthering Heights* (Penguin)
Carr, John Dickson *The Hollow Man* (Penguin)
Chandler, Raymond: *Trouble is my Business* (Penguin)
Collins, Jackie: *Rockstar* (Heinemann)
Conran, Shirley: *Lace* (Sidgwick & Jackson)
Cooper, Jilly: *Lisa & Co* (Arlington Books Ltd)
　Riders (Arlington Books Ltd)

Crichton, Michael: *The Andromeda Strain* (Jonathan Cape)

Dahl, Roald: 'The Way up to Heaven', in *Kiss Kiss* (Michael Joseph)

Dickens, Charles: *A Christmas Carol* (Routledge & Kegan Paul)

Doubtfire, Dianne: Kick a Tin Can (out of print)
The Wrong Face (W. H. Allen)

Doyle, Roddy: *The Commitments* (Heinemann)

du Maurier, Daphne: *The Birds* (Victor Gollancz)
Jamaica Inn (Victor Gollancz)
My Cousin Rachel (Victor Gollancz)
Rebecca (Victor Gollancz)

Duncan, Lois: Stranger with My Face (Hamish Hamilton)
The Twisted Window (Hamish Hamilton)

Ellin, Stanley: *The Man from Nowhere* (Jonathan Cape)

Ellis, Alice Thomas: *The Birds of the Air* (Gerald Duckworth)
The Other Side of the Fire (Gerald Duckworth)

Ellman, Lucy: *Sweet Desserts* (Virago Press)

Follett, Ken: *The Eye of the Needle* (Futura)

Forstchen, William R.: *Rally Cry* (Penguin)

Forster, E. M.: *A Room with a View* (Edward Arnold)

Forster, Margaret: *Have the Men had Enough?* (Chatto & Windus)

Forsyth, Frederick: *The Day of the Jackal* (Century Hutchinson)

Fowles, John: *The French Lieutenant's Woman* (Jonathan Cape)

Francis, Dick: *Dead Cert* (Michael Joseph)
Twice Shy (Michael Joseph)

Fraser, George MacDonald: *Flashman* (Herbert Jenkins Ltd)

Frayn, Michael: *A Very Private Life* (HarperCollins)

Gallico, Paul: *The Poseidon Adventure* (Heinemann)

Golding, William: *Lord of the Flies* (Faber & Faber)

Grisham, John: *The Firm* (Century)
The Pelican Brief (Century)

Hailey, Arthur: *Airport* (Michael Joseph)

Haran, Maeve: *Having it All* (Michael Joseph)

Hardy, Thomas: *Far from the Madding Crowd* (Macmillan)
The Mayor of Casterbridge (Macmillan)

Harris, Ruth Elwyn: *The Silent Shore* (Julia MacRae Books)

Hart, Josephine: *Damage* (Chatto & Windus)
Sin (Chatto & Windus)

Hartley, L. P.: *The Go-Between* (Hamish Hamilton)

Highsmith, Patricia: *The Talented Mr Ripley* (The Cresset Press)

Howatch, Susan: *Cashelmara* (Hamish Hamilton)
    Penmarric (Hamish Hamilton)
Irving, John: *A Son of the Circus* (Bloomsbury)
James, Henry: *The Turn of the Screw* (Penguin)
James, P. D.: *A Taste for Death* (Faber & Faber)
Keillor, Garrison: *Happy to be Here* (Faber & Faber)
    Lake Wobegon Days (Faber & Faber)
    'Post Office';, in *Leaving Home* (Faber & Faber)
Kellerman, Jonathan: *Silent Partner* (Macdonald)
King, Stephen: *Carrie* (New English Library)
    It (Hodder & Stoughton)
    The Stand (Doubleday, USA)
Koontz, Dean: *The Bad Place* (Headline)
Lawrence, D. H.: *The Plumed Serpent* (Heinemann)
    Sons and Lovers (Penguin)
Leonard, Elmore: *City Primeval* (W. H. Allen)
    Glitz (Viking)
Lodge, David: *Changing Places* (Secker & Warburg)
    Nice Work (Secker & Warburg)
Lovesey, Peter: *The Last Detective* (Scribners Press)
Ludlum, Robert: *The Parsifal Mosaic* (Bantam Books, USA)
McCammon, Robert: *Boy's Life* (Michael Joseph)
McCullough, Colleen: *The Thornbirds* (Futura)
MacDonald, John D.: *The Dreadful Lemon Sky*
    (Ballantine Books, USA), from his Travis McGee Series
McInerney, Jay: *Bright Lights, Big City* (Jonathan Cape)
Maclean, Alistair: *Night Without End* (HarperCollins)
    Where Eagles Dare (HarperCollins)
Mansfield, Katherine: 'The Fly', in *The Dove's Nest and Other Stories*
    (Century Hutchinson)
Mantel, Hilary: *Vacant Possession* (Chatto & Windus)
Mather, Anne: *Duelling Fire* (Mills & Boon)
Mitchell, Margaret: *Gone with the Wind* (Macmillan)
Moggach, Deborah: *Close to Home* (HarperCollins)
Nabokov, Vladimir: *Lolita* (Weidenfeld & Nicolson)
Orwell, George: *Nineteen Eighty-Four* (Secker & Warburg)
Pronzoni, Bill: 'Proof of Guilt', in *Ellery Queen's Mystery Magazine*
Proust, Marcel: *Remembrance of Things Past* (Chatto & Windus)
Rendell, Ruth: *Demon in my View* (Century Hutchinson)
Salinger, J. D.: *The Catcher in the Rye* (Hamish Hamilton)

Bibliography

Seton, Anya: *Foxfire* (Hodder & Stoughton)
Shakespeare, William: *Romeo and Juliet* (Penguin)
Shelley, Mary: *Frankenstein* (J. M. Dent)
Smith, Murray: *Devil's Juggler* (Michael Joseph)
Smith, Scott: *A Simple Plan* (Viking)
Steinbeck, John: *East of Eden* (Pan)
Stevenson, Robert Louis: *The Strange Case of Dr Jekyll and Mr Hyde*
    (Macdonald)
Thomas, Rosie: *Other People's Marriages* (Michael Joseph)
Trollope, Joanna: *The Spanish Lover* (Bloomsbury)
Turow, Scott: *Presumed Innocent* (Bloomsbury)
Vine, Barbara: *A Dark-Adapted Eye* (Viking)
    A Fatal Inversion (Viking)
Walters, Minette: *The Ice House* (Macmillan)
Waugh, Evelyn: *Brideshead Revisited* (Penguin)
Whitney, Phyllis A.: *Vermilion* (Heinemann)
Wyndham, John: *The Day of the Triffids* (Heinemann)
Zahavi, Helen: *Dirty Weekend* (HarperCollins)

Index

About the Author

Margret Geraghty regularly contributes creative writing features to *Writing* magazine and *Writers' News*. She is a published author, runs classes in creative writing and is a Literature Assesor for Southern Arts. Margret lives in Winchester.